I0421933

NOBODY KNOWS
"A gay man's experience"

By Z. E. Arlea

Nobody Knows
"A gay man's experience"

Published by: The Male Box
Copyright © 2009 The Male Box
Cover design by: JR Richardson and Z. E. Arlea
Cover Photo by: Digital Innovation Designs
Interior design by: Digital Innovation Designs

This book is a work of fiction. The names, characters, places, and incidents are products of the writer's imagination or have been used fictitiously and are not to be construed as real. Any resemblance to persons, living or dead, actual events, locale or organizations is entirely coincidental.

All Rights Are Reserved. No part of this book may be used or reproduced in any manner whatsoever without written permission, except in the case of brief quotations embodied in critical articles and reviews.

First paperback edition, December 2009

ISBN 978-0-557-21198-2

www.themale-box.com

"If you want to know your past - look into your present conditions. If you want to know your future - look into your present actions."

Chinese Proverb

Table of Contents

Dedication 8

Letter from the author 9

Introduction 11

Childhood 13

Challenges 17

Self Acceptance 25

Learning the gay life 29

The wild side – A collection of erotic sex experiences.

- I willingly took it 33
- The Best Room Service 40
- Weekend at Michael's house 45
- David and I 50
- My Consultant 55
- Twice a charm 59
- Happy Birthday 65
- Not so straight after all 75
- It was only a dream 80
- What's Love got to do with it? 84
- In the office 90

Looking for Love 99

Is it love? 110

About the author 117

Coming Soon!

Dedication

This book is dedicated to Akil who has been such an inspiration and very instrumental in helping me change my life in many ways he doesn't even know. Also, I dedicate this book to my two best friends Fefe and San, who have been the greatest motivators and to my editor Jordan, whose friendship I am most grateful for. Finally I can't forget all my online friends who everyday continue to play an important part in my life.

LETTER FROM THE AUTHOR

Dear Readers,

My journey from experiencing what you will read in this book "Nobody Knows – A gay man's experience," has been one of pain, sadness, joy, shame, remorse, regret, laughter, anger, and finally peace. I have come to understand over time that all of my life experiences were meant to follow the path that it did.

Almost a year ago I began reflecting on my life experiences, in particular my lifestyle. Looking back it is hard to believe how so many years could pass by and I didn't notice. It feels like just yesterday I was going to high school. (Damn, I feel old).

Since I was a child, my desire has always been to share my life story. I began writing my autobiography at the age of nineteen. People often asked me why would I write my autobiography at such a young age, how much "life" did I possibly live to write about? Little did they know I lived an extremely eventful life, or as the guys would say, a life filled with drama.

At the age of twenty I completed writing my autobiography. For me writing the book was easy but reading it over was the difficult part. While reading, I felt like I was living through the experiences again, even more than when I was writing about them. I was overwhelmed with emotions during this process. When I was finished, I realized that I had failed to include anything in the book about my personal lifestyle. Because of this I decided to write the untold story…the story behind the story.

I began to prepare myself to write. What I would usually do is write down my aim for the book and what message I want to bring across to my readers. In the process I wanted to test myself. I gave myself two weeks, exactly fourteen days to complete the entire book. I stocked up on food and for the fourteen days I placed myself under personal house arrest.

Like most first time authors, I was filled with hope and despair. Excitement filled my soul. And for the fourteen days it was difficult for me to sleep. I just wanted to complete this book. At most I would sleep for four hours during 7am and 11am. My biological clock was messed up and even after the manuscript was completed I still could not sleep at night.

Now that I have fulfilled the task of completing this chapter of my life, it is my hope that this book inspires and entertains you. I wanted to freely express myself in my writing hence you will find the book to be very raw and erotic.

I would appreciate if you would drop me a line of feedback after reading this book. It is my humble hope that you will find my writing enjoyable and revealing of a place and time that stood still in my heart and memories. I am eternally grateful for your support and interest in my story.

With love,

Z. E. Arlea

Introduction

My life is simple and my wants are few, so why am I so unhappy? By almost anyone's reckoning my existence is pretty tame and uneventful. I want to be the first to admit that it is not so. Also, I must admit most people really don't know me at all. I have lots of secrets. I live two lives, a secret life that only I and a few others know about and the life that most people know about, the so-called *normal* life of a young man growing up. I have by no means ever been the kind of guy to open his heart to just anyone. So if you think you know, you have no idea. In the past I have sold myself as being an extremely strong minded and courageous individual but really and truly I was a very shy guy that would often wear a mask in public just to appear brave.

Being the type of guy I am, I am very careful when making friends. I often wonder if they will accept me for who I am or for who I pretend to be. The few friends I do have all say to me that I should get out more, meet more people. I know they are right, however, after all this time by myself I can't seem to get past the self doubt and the lack of experience and fear of acceptance. Perhaps I am making this too difficult on myself; perhaps it is easier than I think.

I know you are probably questioning who I am; I want you to know that you know me very well. You see me every day, as soon as you walk out the house. Sometimes I am the first guy you see when you get up in the morning. Do you know who I am now? I am your husband, your brother, your best friend, your roommate, your father, your doctor or even your lawyer. I am your cousin, your carpenter, the delivery boy and your pastor. I am the bank teller, your child's teacher, and I am even your part time lover. Are you still questioning who I am? Haven't you found it out yet? Okay, I will tell you, I AM GAY.

I don't necessarily like that label. I believe I am just human and that's enough labeling for me. Most times all anyone ever sees of gays on TV are the one-sided media stereotypes; the queens, the half-naked Pride marchers, or the in-your-face loud mouths. That isn't me. I'm just a regular guy who likes men.

I have lived most of my life learning or trying to accept and love myself for who I am, what I am and why I am. I have had my share of challenges and struggles along the way. Nevertheless, I have learned to accept, I have learned to overcome and I have also learned to love. It was not easy and still isn't easy. However, I am happy to be able to say, for once in my life, I like who I am, I have pride in myself and I accept myself.

CHILDHOOD

My theory is that the hardest work anyone does in life is to appear normal.

From the movie Ed TV

It is much easier to break a good habit rather than to break the bad. Everyone has battles, challenges or whatever you would like to call it. For some it is their eating habits, others it is saving money, for me it is my sexuality. For many years I have been battling with my self, trying to learn how to love and accept myself for who I am. For as long as I know myself my life has been all about pleasing others and making myself unhappy.

Who am I? What am I? Why am I? I really don't know. But what I know now is this, whoever I am, whatever I am, why I am, will no longer affect me. I refuse to continue living a life of pain and suffering to make others happy. Love me as I am, or don't love me at all, that is the new policy I have developed for myself.

I am 24 years old and even though I have over one hundred thousand dollars in bills, I feel most comfortable and happy about myself, about life, than I have ever felt before.

I was brought up in a predominantly anti gay environment where gays were treated with repugnance. With the greatest fear I kept my life private or even tried to suppress my feelings hoping that one day it will go away. My parents are both devout Christians and would disown me or even go as far as to physically abuse me if they were to find out. I often questioned myself if people really know what love is. How could you love me because I am your son but hate me because I am emotionally and sexually attracted to guys? It is really confusing.

I am the last son of my parents, after me are only girls. Being the youngest boy I was forced to hang with the girls because my older siblings would refuse to be around the younger ones or would usually be outdoors. The younger ones did not have the privilege of going outside so we had to resort to indoor games such as board games and dolly house. I am not going to say that my lifestyle is a result of me playing with my sisters and dolls when I was younger. I believe it is a sequence of experiences that have brought me to this point in my life.

I was the more sheltered child being the youngest boy. I was also what some people would call a pretty boy, very good-looking or having more female features and tendencies growing up. Because of this I would be called girly-boy sometimes by my brother and even by fellow class-mates in school. The name calling I must say, affected me psychologically. As a result I went through my school days with few friends.

At the age of eight, I had my first gay experience. I was only a child and was unaware of the gravity of the experience at that time. A friend of my family, male, about sixteen years, asked me to play with him in my dad's car. Me being young and oblivious to what was going to happen, I got into the car. This friend of the family, let's call him Mr. X, asked me to take my clothes off. Without asking a question I removed my clothing. He then began to play with my penis. I must admit the feeling was…interesting. But at that age I didn't know better. He then asked me to return the favor which I did. Mr. X then made an attempt to insert his finger into my anus but it was so painful he had to stop. He told me never to tell what had happened. I was afraid that I would get into serious trouble so I decided to tell my caretaker's daughter, Rena, who was around my age. Rena then told her mother given that she was the only adult present. My caretaker advised me by no means to make mention of it to anyone in life again. It has remained my lifelong secret.

NOBODY KNOWS

Growing up as a teenager I had my share of girlfriends. I have been in puppy-love relationships at school. I can recall being sexually aroused by girls during the age of eleven to fifteen, but around the age of fifteen or sixteen something happened. My feelings towards the opposite sex had depleted. I don't know how, I don't know why, all I knew was the feeling I had for girls was no more. I realized this when I was watching soft porn in my bedroom. I would stay up very late at night to look at soft porn, on Cinemax and HBO. While watching the movies I became conscious that the guys' bodies, appealed to me more than the women. I would even touch myself imagining that the guy in the movie was making love to me the way they were making love to the woman. It was around that time I experienced my very first orgasm and in actuality understood what masturbation was.

It was a quiet night I remember and I was home alone. Exams were drawing near so I should have been studying. Earlier that afternoon I had visited a friend's house and saw a VHS tape with no label. In those days any VHS tape without a label would usually be porn. I immediately stole it putting it in my bag fearful that I would be caught, I wasn't. When I got home I went directly to my room giving the impression that I would be studying for my forthcoming exams. As soon as I entered the room and closed the door I hooked up the VCR and inserted the tape, turning the television volume down to the lowest. I sat back and began looking at, for the first time in my life, hard core porn. I was flabbergasted!

The raw sight of the men's dicks turned me on so much I began to touch my self. I took off all my clothing while sitting on the edge of the bed in absolute pleasure rubbing my eight inch dick as if I was thrusting in and out of someone. I was literally fucking my hand. I could feel pre-cum on the head of my dick every time I rubbed it. It was the hardest I had ever felt my cock, even harder than my customary morning hard on. This was strange but it was also very electrifying. I began stroking myself feverishly as the feeling of pleasure and excitement intensified. While stroking my dick I can only wonder what was about to happen. I could feel some sort of tension welling up in my stomach but wasn't sure if that was what I was striving to achieve or not. My hands began to get tired but I refused to stop as the feeling was so great. I actually thought I might have been hurting myself because the feeling in my stomach and groin had become so intense that I couldn't move. While Stroking my dick with my right hand I took my left hand and began to rub my testicles, at that point I could feel allot of pressure building up. I could tell that something was about to happen. My breathing increased rapidly and I began to groan uncontrollably as my sexual excitement grew more intense. Just then, I released a rather surprisingly huge amount of cum. It shot out so hard that it flew across a ten foot room and splattered halfway up the wall. That was the first shot and the rest just kept coming out over and over with every shot making my legs weaker and weaker. I continued squeezing my balls while I stroked my cock back and forth with every pulse, the milky white ooze just kept blasting out of me. Afterwards, I was so shocked and drained by then that I had to sit down before I fell down. The feeling was incredible.

From that day on masturbating became a part of my daily activities. On week days I would masturbate every night before I went to bed and on weekends if I was home alone I would spend lots of time masturbating. It became a hobby. The fact that my hands have never been confused over how it felt about my dick, and my dick always knew the touch, made me feel like every time was just as good as the first. I was surprised that I could actually give myself such pleasure. The strange thing for me was when ever I came I felt contented and drained. The orgasm was a trip. I always wanted more. A shameful pasttime I could not stop.

During that same year something happened that would change my life. I found God. I began going to church often and made a conscious decision to change my life. I decided to stop looking at pornography and for a few years I had avoided all literature, movies and other situations which could arouse homosexual lust.

I went as far as deleting all the channels that would possibly broadcast anything that might wrongly influence me. I thought to myself by making that change in my life I would one day reach a point of happiness. I believed in my heart that by changing my life for God would be good, but why was I still unhappy?

CHALLENGES

Labels are for filing. Labels are for clothing. Labels are not for people. - Martina Navratilova

As a child growing up and even as an adult I faced several challenges. These experiences or challenges helped to form who I am today.

From an early age I was a victim of name calling. Some people may think it's a simple stage in growing up where kids would call each other names, for me it was one of the more depressing aspects of growing up. I was a child that was forced to survive my school days in the face of all too frequent taunts based on the way I spoke, my intelligence, and my questionable sexual orientation or gender expression. It was difficult because not only did I have to deal with this at school but at home as well from my siblings. I can remember my brothers teasing me. They would call me girl, gay, queer and all kind of names. They would sometimes even do it in front of their friends, making their friends feel comfortable to do the same.

For many years as a child growing up I was wounded by the name calling. As I got older I came to realize that negative labels and insults have the potential to truly hurt a child's feelings. Children who are frequently insulted by their siblings often remember the experience with pain even in adulthood. And this is exactly what happened to me. However, remembered pain is not the worse consequence of name-calling. For me, far worse was the impact name-calling had on the development of my personality. I can recall during my childhood being called names that left me truly believing that I was damaged, useless, bad and defective, as well as unlovable. Even as an adult I would feel less adequate, less competent and worthless the more I think of the insults.

This effect is much more powerful in childhood when a child's sense of self is not yet fully formed. Once I began entertaining such notions about myself, I began acting in ways that were consistent with that poor self-image. The labeling for me was crippling. It even affected the number of friends I had growing up. I forced myself to learn how to be happy without having any friends or someone to talk to. Although I was surrounded by people at all times, I never really had anyone with whom I felt comfortable enough to confide in or to even call a friend and because of this I guess some people saw me as an easy victim.

****

I was 17 years travelling overseas. I was staying in a hotel alone and even though I had family living close by; I chose to stay on my own because I enjoyed the independence. One day my cousin invited me to accompany him to the beach. While at the beach a very handsome guy walked up to me with a welcoming smile on his face. He looked like he was about 23 years old, with an athletic body.

He introduced himself as Carl. Carl was apparently solo on the beach and wanted company. Of course I did not mind being in his company since my cousin was busy drinking every beer he could get his hands on. Carl and I spoke for quite sometime until it was growing quite dark and I decided to head back to my hotel. I said my goodbyes and departed.

Carl however, insisted that I took a walk with him. I did not mind because he appeared to be cool. We walked for quite some time and then he asked "Do you like me?"

I was in total shock because I was never asked that question by a guy before.

"No, well…I mean…, you seem to be cool, you're a nice guy, I like you, but not in any wrong way," I replied, embarrassed.

At that point I could tell he knew I was mentally strained by his question.

"It's okay if you like me, nothing wrong with that, because I really like you," He then looked into my eyes and said.

At that point I realized that he was gay. I was very nervous but I was also very excited by the fact that I was talking to a gay guy for the first time in my life. I asked him several questions. A short walk turned out to be a long walk into a deserted area. He then asked me to go back to his place with him. Already I felt a great level of comfort in his presence and thought that it would be okay to go back to his place.

As we got to his apartment I learned that he lived alone and worked in a nearby hotel. He then insisted I take a bath as we were on the beach all day. Honestly, I felt a little uncomfortable about his request but I did not want to come across as scared so I went along with it. While in the bathroom I asked Carl to hand me a towel. As I stepped out the bathroom the unthinkable happened.

Carl grabbed my arms and pushed me down on the bed. To my surprise he was already naked and fully erect. I could not believe that he was about to rape me. I began to fight on the bed as he took his hands and placed them over my mouth preventing me from screaming or even calling out for help. He then placed a pillow over my head making it difficult for me to breath. He began to lick and suck on my nipples and all the while I am on the bed thinking how could I survive being raped.

Suddenly he bit my nipple really hard and I screamed out in pain…as if anyone could hear me with the pillow still over my face. Carl then roughly turned my body over, forcing me to lie down on my stomach. His body was twice the size of mine and he was way stronger than I. So as much as I tried to fight him off, he was in total control. I began to cry and begged him to stop; he paid no attention to my words, his focus was solely on planting my body down on the bed to get inside of me.

Without a doubt, I knew what was coming next, Carl was about to fuck the life out of me. He had me totally pinned down on the bed; the only part of my body I could move at that point was my fingers and toes.

"You are not going to enjoy this," Carl then whispered in my ears.

Without any lubrication or condoms he rammed his entire dick inside of me. My entire body went into shock and became motionless. I had no choice. I just lay there as he fucked my ass mercilessly, without any emotion. As he continued ramming his dick into me I could feel the blood running down my legs.

I just cried, feeling sorry for myself, hoping and praying that it will all be over soon. He continued for about fifteen minutes. Suddenly I felt his entire body resting on top of mine as he fucked harder and harder. He then started to bite my back as he shoved himself into me. Out of the blue he gave off a loud moan and I felt him orgasm inside of me. Carl got off of my seemingly lifeless body and went into the bathroom. I was so afraid of him retuning from the bathroom with the intention of fucking me again, I scrambled for my clothes, opened the door as naked as I was born and ran out of the apartment as fast as, if not faster than a cheetah in pursuit of food. I put on my clothing by the road side and ran for a few miles back to the hotel. When I got into the hotel room, I closed the windows, checked the door locks, and withdrew to the safety or at the least the seclusion, of the small hotel room. I then took a very long shower allowing the water to run over my body. I cleaned myself off and went to bed. That night and for several nights after, I could not sleep. I was too scared to turn off the light in my room. I had to keep reminding myself that I was grateful to be alive, but I also kept wondering how God could allow such awful things to happen to people. I often questioned how I would move forward with my life after having such an experience. A few times I dozed off and dreamt someone was in the room, and would jump out of bed, frightened. I wondered if I would ever sleep soundly again. I couldn't fathom it at all. In total bewilderment I literally sat in my room for the next few days that followed crying or feeling sorry for myself. I never shared this experience with anyone because I was afraid people would say I went looking for it.

Rape is an attack on body, mind, and spirit. In my case my spirit was wounded even more profoundly than my body. It is the invisible wounds that are most hard to understand. They are still painful during the weeks, months, or years after being raped. Recovery for me was a difficult process. When I thought that healing was not possible I learned that it is not only possible but it is also unbelievably rewarding.

For me time, support, reading books and talking with understanding people were essential to overcoming the pain - mental, emotional and spiritual. It took years for me to get through that full healing process, but fortunately I did.

Before I went through the healing process I went through a state of serious depression. I hated myself, hated everyone and everything around me. All I wanted to do was die. I was suffering with serious depression, anxiety, peer pressure and low self-esteem. All of this caused me to display serious self-injurious behaviors; I had major problems understanding personal changes, knowing where to fit in and worst of all I had a terrible relationship with my parents and siblings.

After being raped all I could think about was committing suicide. I did not think my life was worth living anymore. I began to have thoughts on how to commit suicide. I knew that I was very discouraged because the events in my life were not going in the direction that I wanted or expected them to.

I started to ask myself several questions. Is there a God? Does anyone even care? Why am I here? If God loves me why is he allowing all of this to happen to me? I had more questions than answers. I felt like I had no choice but to deal with this on my own and the best way to deal with all my problems was to put a complete stop to them...by committing suicide.

Menacing thoughts began entering my head. I was only thinking about ways to commit suicide. I began to research the internet for websites on how to tie the right knot to create a noose. I often wondered if the branches of the tree in the back yard were strong or high enough to hang myself. Would I have the physical capability to accomplish such a feat? I just could not stop thinking about it. And no one knew what was going through my mind. The thought of everything was frightening but I was determined to do it.

As time went by the thoughts became more insistent. It was as if these thoughts had a life of their own, a separate entity, that had somehow taken residence inside my brain. I was starting to get worried and wondered if I needed help. I was not moving beyond this and the horrifying thoughts were only getting worse!

I became so distant from everyone even my only two friends Fefe and San. They often questioned what was wrong with me. I refused to share. I kept my feelings, my thoughts, my anguish and my pain all to myself. I thought they were too horrific to share, with anyone. No one would have ever believed what was going on in my head was really me, because they were more familiar with my false, happy, outgoing personality. I was afraid to tell people for fear that they would minimize my feelings and make me feel ashamed or even worse than I already felt about myself and life. They might reject me and I couldn't deal with those reactions. I was trying so hard to cope with what was happening to me. I wanted to be strong. I wanted to believe in God. I tried very hard to think positively. Maybe I could purge that terrifying intruder who had begun to reside in my brain, I often wondered.

I attempted to deal with the depression on my own, but the insistent voice became stronger. I reached a point where I finally figured out a method of suicide and wondered how I should phrase the suicide note that I would leave for my family. One part of my brain mulled these thoughts in a totally irrational manner while the more rational part of my brain knew suicide was wrong and that it would destroy my family. It was almost as though there were two individuals inside me - the person controlled by this persistent voice and the other part of me that loved God and believed that he did have a good plan for my life in spite of the painful trial in which I was so deeply immersed.

It was the two days before my eighteenth birthday when I decided to call my aunt who I felt most comfortable with to talk about what was going on in my life. I called her at around eight in the evening asking to stop by her house, letting her know I had a very serious problem and I needed someone to talk to. She told me to stop by at eight the next morning. I got there about ten minutes to eight but she was not at home. I tried opening the front door which she usually left open if she stepped out and was expecting to return shortly. The door was locked.

Nothing could have been worse. The moment I decided to talk to someone and seek help they were not there for me. I felt like there was no hope and I decided to end my life right there and then. Sitting on the porch with paper and a pen in hand, I began to write my suicide note. With tears in my eyes I began writing. The person controlled by this insistent voice had my entire body now but somehow the part of me that loved God and believed that he had a superior plan for my life was still fighting to keep me alive.

Suddenly a voice in my head told me to try opening the front door again. As I approached the front door already I could sense the sudden difference in the way I was feeling. As I put my hands on the door handle to turn it the door mysteriously opened on its own. For you reading this it might seem to be a normal door opening but for me it was like God opened a door for me. From that day on I looked at my life in a totally different way and never thought of suicide again.

Knowing what is happening in my life went a long way in being able to regain control over my life and my emotions. For me real healing could never have been possible until the depression was lifted. In my case, a locked door mysteriously opening before my eyes gave me a sense of hope, some confirmation of there being a higher being that wanted to get my attention. This made me feel better about myself, I felt like I had someone's attention and for once someone really cared.

As I got older I came to realize that suicide was only one of the many challenges I have had to face as a part of growing up. I have been aware that I was gay around age sixteen. But my greatest fear of all was to admit it to my family, friends and the general public who have been questioning my sexuality for most of my life.

I have several friends who have said to me that a parent always knows if their child is gay. My parents have never asked me a question about my sexuality. Sometimes I wonder if it's because they are in denial. They have never seen me with a girl and thinking about it, they have never even seen me with friends. I am so private about my life that I would not even have a friend over.

Because of the culture I was brought up in, the religion or faith I was trained to believe in and the point of view that my family and friends had, I was completely afraid that coming out will completely end my relationship with my family and friends.

Even though most people coming out today don't necessarily or fully understand how bad the stigma associated with being gay was as little as ten years ago, the little community that I came from is still ten years behind. Culturally, the world in general is making progress to better accept gays; however, where I am from they continue to maintain their stance and will not accept it at all.

I was faced with a complicated decision in my life, either come out or hide for the rest of my life. At one time I decided to try to suppress my feelings totally. I withdrew myself from everyone and everything that I considered "gay". That lasted only a few months and for those few months I was very unhappy. I began feeling depressed again with no one to talk to and unaware of what to do. Once again I was fighting with myself and this time it was a losing battle. It was not a choice between life and death. It was a choice of me being who I am and accepting myself or trying to be something I wasn't and hating myself for it.

SELF ACCEPTANCE

It is not easy to find happiness in ourselves, and it is not possible to find it elsewhere. - Agnes Repplier

To me self acceptance is to love and be happy with who you are. Some call it self-esteem, others refer to it as self-love, but whatever it is called, one thing I do know is that the feeling of accepting yourself is great. I came to the realization that when I accept myself, I form an agreement with myself to appreciate, validate, accept and support who I am.

When I first began to be aware that I needed to accept myself and love myself first, before I can develop any meaningful relationships with others, I realized that I did not know where to start. I had never accepted myself before. I did not know what I really wanted in life and out of a relationship. While learning or discovering myself I realized that knowing me meant getting to know myself on a physical, emotional and spiritual level, as well as getting to know what I was looking for in a potential relationship partner. Before even getting to the point of searching for a life partner, I began questioning myself about my values, goals, lifestyle choices, and the type of individuals with whom I would like to share my life's journey.

Day by day, the majority of us fight a painful war with our inner selves. It is a constant battle. For me, it has been my sexuality. As stated in the first chapter, I have battled with it for all my life with the fear that someone will find out. Because of this there is an increase in the constant criticism, pressure, anger, sadness and endless cruel comparisons. It is an everyday struggle that gets in the way and keeps me from seeing myself for who I really am and from achieving or fulfilling my true purpose in life. Where did this war begin and why?

The answer to that question can be found in a well-known and very often used word: Self-Esteem. Self-Esteem is the way you look at and feel about yourself. If I am always fighting with myself and feeding myself thoughts that make me feel less valuable or not as important or attractive as other people, then I am suffering from Low Self-Esteem.

I realized that even though I was a brave, self motivated, strong minded individual, I still had a very low self-esteem, and I think that developed as a result of fear my family would hate me if they were to find out about my lifestyle, as well as the emotional teasing and turmoil I went through as a child.

To really come to terms with my self, I decided to put myself through a few months of personal development. During those months I read numerous books and spoke to several friends who have had their share of experiences and have since grown to be comfortable with themselves. Their advice really helped. I was soon becoming a best friend to myself instead of an enemy.

I remember there were times I would look in the mirror and speak to reflection saying that I would no longer feel sorry for myself and that I have the power and strength to feel and be happy, confident and successful, and I will do it because I am valuable and deserving of it, just as anyone else. Reassuring myself everyday was a big key to staying focused and improving the way I felt about me and the life I live.

Another essential lesson I had to teach myself while discovering me was to stop comparing myself to others. I came to accept that we are all created different and unique and possess talents and qualities that no one else has and will never have, and that is something to take pride in and love about yourself. Once I had received official approval and acceptance of myself from myself, I realized that everything and everyone else around me will do the same.

After discovering myself I knew that to make me complete, well, not totally complete, but at least to feel happier I needed to remove one feeling that has been controlling my emotions for sometime. This was a great feeling of loneliness.

I was a victim of rape, suicidal thoughts and depression and loving me was something I had never learned. How was I to love myself? I often wondered. I had already spent thousands of dollars going to psychologists and that never helped. Nothing changed. I still felt hopeless and worthless.

With the desire to love myself and with the belief in the "seek and you shall find" theory, I went in search of a method to help me love myself. In my quest I came across a book, *Chicken Soup for the Young Adult Soul*, which changed my life forever. In the book I found stories of people around my age that were facing similar challenges as me. For the first time in my life I felt like I was not alone.

I began making notes and started focusing on loving me, fixing me and making me happy. Learning to accept and love myself started with making a conscious decision, an intention to become happy and lead a fulfilled life. I realized that when I do not love myself, as a result of suffering from low self esteem, I found that it was impossible to ever reach the potential that I am capable of. Making a decision to love myself was really saying to myself that I was ready to come alive. I began to accept that I was responsible for the outcomes that I experienced in life.

Accepting me became a mission that had to be accomplished. While looking back on my life, my experiences and the various changes that affected me, I came to understand that over the years I have used my lack of acceptance which, for me was punishment, abuse, name calling and being friendless, as a motivation to get me to do or not to do, to be and not to be what I think I should be and should do. Today I believe that by accepting myself for who I am I can become more of who I want to be.

A friend once asked me, why I would say I accept myself yet still I am afraid to come out. I personally don't think coming out means that I need to wear a t-shirt saying I'm coming out or I am gay and proud. I think coming out means no longer being dishonest to yourself, no longer hiding your feelings, no longer being afraid to express your love to the same sex. At the end of the day, however you view "coming out" the important thing for me is to respect myself.

This entire process was very difficult, from accepting that you are gay to openly being gay. We all have seen the movies, TV shows, read the books, and heard from friends the horror stories. We do not know what it will be like for ourselves until we do it. I personally believe that my sexual preference is my personal business and if I don't wish to share it with anyone, for any reason, that too is my business. However, the important thing is what ever I do, how ever I do it, where ever I do it, I must ensure that I am happy about it. At the end of the day it is up to me to decide who I am willing to share my personal life with.

I have read several books, spoken to thousands of people about the subject of homosexuality. Based on all my experience, today I can honestly say that I believe being gay isn't good or bad, right or wrong. It just is. I grew to accept myself for who and what I am. As we all know in everything there is always room for improvement, however, at this point in my life I am not only comfortable, content and happy but I am also fearless of what people think about my sexuality. If asked about my sexuality I will never say I am gay, only because I don't believe in labels. I once read a quotation by Martina Navratilova which says "Labels are for filing, Labels are for clothing, Labels are not for people". I totally agree with that.

Learning the gay life

Is life not a hundred times too short for us to stifle ourselves? -
Friedrich Nietzsche

Most people say that when you first come out into the gay community you are wild; you want to experience everything, you are still searching for yourself, wanting to find out your likes and dislikes. Some people disagree, I must admit I agree.

At the point of acceptance I wanted to find myself. I was at a crossroad, a turning point with an unpredictable outcome, where I just wanted to try anything and everything. I think it's fair to say that a lot of gay guys have been at that point.

I began reading books and surfing the internet seeking information about gay dating, even though I did not think to myself that I could possibly date a guy where I lived. The environment was too dead set against gays. I even researched how gay sex should be done properly. Growing up I heard so much negative and false things about homosexuality for example, where I came from people would usually say if you're gay (fucking in your bottom) you can't drink soup because it would run straight out of you. Funny enough being ignorant to the facts I was lead to believe. Even when I was raped, it took me weeks if not months before I drank soup. It's only until I began chatting with gay guys online and asking questions I learned and was able to correct so many misconceptions I had in my head about the homosexual lifestyle.

After reading and learning so much about the lifestyle I was in a hurry to find myself a boyfriend, someone I could have sex with. I wanted to experience anal intercourse so much that I made several attempts to finger myself. At first the feeling was weird but as time went by I grew to love the feeling of having my finger or fingers inside of me. Overtime my fingers were just not enough and I wanted to feel more, I wanted to feel the real thing inside of me, a real dick.

I began trying the dating thing. As I said it would not have been easy to date a guy where I lived so I started off dating guys online. I found it to be really difficult being gay and finding love. I think I was going about it the wrong way. The "How To Find a Man" book I read was of no help. I guess this process needed a non systematic approach.

I thought to myself that first of all, it was most important to market myself. As a gay guy I began to really consider the image I projected. I think this is something not just for gays wanting to find a date but also for anyone, woman to woman or even man to woman. I believe that people attract the type of person who is attracted to the signs you are sending out.

It's around this time I realized how much drama you can find in the gay community. I remember going out with guys for the first time. I must admit I am a looker, well at lease so I have been told. Unusually when I go out, which is not that often, most guys I meet would want to get to know me and this is where the "dramas" come in. In the gay community people often believe that if they see you talking to someone, you are sleeping with them. Well if that was the case, I slept with over one hundred thousand guys. Rumors began to go around. People were talking. The word in town was that the new guy is sleeping around. Well I must admit I had my share of do ups (making out with guys). But I thank God I can still count the amount of guys I have had sex with. Most people found that hard to believe, but it is true.

I must confess I can be very flirtatious. I think it is part of my nature and to my advantage I had a way with words. I could easily persuade guys into getting what I want and how I wanted it. Something I use it to my advantage, unaware at the time that I was just hurting myself in the process.

As I learned more about the gay life I concluded that it was best for me to limit the amount of friends I had in the community and also the amount of guys I talk to. I remember meeting guys who I thought was really cool, only to find out that they were living a lie. These guys were like the stereotypical man, they would lie to get anything especially to get in your pants.

I began to hate the gay life. It was not what I thought it to be. My perception was that gays were loving people and if I had a gay relationship it would be way better than a straight one. In my head I thought I could find perfection in a gay relationship. It was only when I became part of the community the reality hit and subsequently I realized all that I fantasized about was only my hopes and dream, it was not reality.

Like in the real world, within the gay community very few are to be trusted. I could remember sharing an apartment with a guy who at that point I considered to be a really good friend. Several times we would make out. Thank God it never got to sex. Only to find out months later that he was HIV positive. We had been friends for years and decided to rent together. We shared secrets, cried on each other's shoulders and still he deceived me because of personal satisfaction. This just goes to show how no one is to be trusted. Fortunately after being tested I was HIV negative.

Even after all my experiences before accepting that I was gay, learning to live with myself, and learning about the gay life and the challenges I would be forced to deal with being in such a community, I still wanted to experience more. I never got the opportunity to willingly have sex with anyone. I wanted to know what it would be like, feeling the dick running in and out of me, being loved and touched by a man. I was craving for it and I made up my mind the first chance I got I was going to do it.

THE WILD SIDE
A COLLECTION OF EROTIC SEX EXPERIENCES.

Without freedom, no one really has a name
~by Milton Acorda

I willingly took it

After being raped, even though the experience was bad, something inside of me continued to crave a man's love. I wanted to feel a man making love to me. I wanted to know what it was really like, how would it feel, having a dick running in and out of my anus. Well, I would eventually find out and begin to realize how much I love sex.

It was a few weeks before my nineteenth birthday. I had been chatting with this guy, Marcus, online for over a month. He came across as very interesting, stable and honest. The ideal guy I would like to be with. I decided to meet him. When I saw him, he was just as I imagined, handsome, manly and I could tell he had a sexy body. It was not long after I got to find out what he really had under his clothes. We met in the city one afternoon and after having some drinks and talking he invited me back to his home.

When we arrived at his house, right away he directed me into his room. Aware of what was going to happen; I realized that my hands were shaking uncontrollably. I found myself lost for words, not knowing what to say, if to ask a question or what to do. Without saying a word, Marcus came over to me while I was standing in the doorway.

"Nice ass," he whispered to my ear and I froze.

Unable to move, Marcus ran his hands down my chest to my crotch. A cold chill ran through my body as my dick grew and stood at attention. Marcus could tell that I was nervous since my body was literally shaking. He began kissing me and started removing my clothes. His kiss was so passionate, I felt as though I was in love. I was young and stupid and desired love, so anything that came across as love made me weak. When he removed all of my clothing he then began to strip off his. He turned away from me to remove his trousers not allowing me to see his dick. When he was fully naked he wrapped a towel around his waist.

"I would love to fuck that ass", Marcus said to me, this time holding my hips in his massive hands and pressing the huge bulge under his towel up against my bottom.

This is what I came for, but it was happening so fast I was truly terrified at this point. Marcus stood a half a foot taller than my 5' 8" stature and was a solid mass of man compared to my thinner, athletic build.

"I'm going to fuck your ass! Would you like that?" he asked, before I could give an answer, he kissed me again.

"I want suck your cock first!" I whispered as I slowly pulled away from him.

He was a large, muscular guy and it was readily apparent that if he wanted to fuck me there was nothing I could have done to resist his advances if I did deem them unwanted. I was his prisoner in this tiny, dimly lit room until I gave him what he wanted. My hands instinctively reached for the top of his towel and I pulled it open to reveal a thick, 6 inch, flaccid cock. It was not that impressive, I was expecting more from a guy with such a big ego. I guess his big ego is to make up for his short comings. Nevertheless, without hesitation I knelt before him, my face inches from his cock, his musky scent filling my nose. His massive left hand came to rest on the back of my head; his right hand grasped his limp cock lifting it up to my mouth. I tilted my head back, looking up into his face, unable to make out any defining features as he gazed down upon me. I had what I dreamt about, total anonymity.

Looking up at Marcus, I accepted my submissive role, kissed the tip of his cock and whispered to myself, "I'm ready now." Closing my eyes and opening my mouth wide Marcus began to slowly feed me his cock. Within moments of his cock entering my mouth, he grasped my head with both of his enormous hands. I opened my mouth wider and wider to accommodate the slow thrusts of his hips. I relaxed my breathing and began gentle swallowing motions to keep from choking. His cock was now beginning to swell in my mouth cutting off my air supply. In an attempt to placate his deeper thrusts I forced my face into his crotch. My lips wrapping around the base of his cock, my nose stuffed into his nest of pubic hair, he let out a loud groan.

"Oh fuck yeah!" he growled.

With his cock entirely in my mouth his grip became vice-like as his swelling cock began to find its' way down my throat. I fought the urge to pull away for fear of angering him. The moments seemed like an eternity as I suppressed my fear and continued my swallowing motions and shallow breathing. My mouth was completely stuffed with cock and I was now holding my breath as the head of his cock continued down my throat.

"Fuck yes!" he yelled, and quickly withdrew his cock from my mouth.

I choked as he withdrew and fought to catch my breath. On my knees choking and panting, Marcus wrapped his fingers into my hair and pulled my head back forcing me to look at him.

"Now I am going to fuck your ass! Get up!" he commanded.

I slowly stood before him. As I bent over in front of him a wave of shame and lust washed over me.

"Nice!" he hissed, as he ran his hand across my small, soft ass.

Enjoying the caresses of his large hand on my bottom, I bent over as he unzipped a bag from which he retrieved lube and condoms.

He quickly knelt behind me and in one motion his hands spread my bottom wide open, his tongue plunged into the crack of my ass. I fell forward hitting my head on the wall and grabbed the small table next to the bed to prevent me from falling to the floor.

"Ooooooohhh fuck yes!" I shouted as I grasped the edges of the table as hard as I could.

His hot, wet tongue felt incredible, his hands frantically trying to rip my ass open wider and wider as his tongue probed deeper and deeper into my tight hole. Marcus continued his crazed feeding frenzy on my ass, my continual moaning only added to his lust. I spread my legs wider as he buried his face deeper into me, the sounds of wet sucking and slurping echoing within the walls of my room.

Totally lost in ecstasy he began to lick the back of my balls as his finger began a slow, methodical pressing against my tight, wet hole. I shivered as he sucked on my balls, the pain offset by the pleasure I was receiving as he snuck his finger past my tight hole and slid it in and out of my bottom.

"You're ready, get on the bed!" he demanded.

My legs were stiff and I fell onto the bed.

"Get on your back!" he commanded.

As I lay on the bed watching him fumble with a condom I remembered a movie I watched a few days before that had me really horny causing me to finger myself for the first time. Marcus then passed the bottle of lube over to me as if I knew what to do with it. I returned the bottle with an innocent look on my face. I guess he knew at that point that he would be teaching me something new. He began to apply lube to my tingling, wet hole.

"You are a fucking slut aren't you?" he growled as I lay on the bed, legs spread, pulling my ass wide open with both hands to receive his cock.

To me his cock was very small, because I had seen much larger in porn and even the guy who raped me had an enormous cock. I was not a dick specialist but I have seen a lot and his was the smallest of them all.

He crawled onto the bed as I spread my legs even wider, raising my bottom up to meet the rock hard cock. I laid back and tried to calm myself as the swollen head of his cock slowly ran up and down the crack of my ass. I wanted him to fuck me so badly that I pulled my ass as wide open as possible as he searched for my opening. The tip of his cock found its mark and my hole instinctively tightened. I fought the searing pain as he pushed harder to overcome my resistance. Even though I thought his cock was small, my hole being so small and tight I wasn't sure I could take him. With gentle, shallow, thrusting motions he continued to try to force himself inside me. In a fit of lust I raised my bottom up to meet his thrust and let out a long moan as he crowned within me.

"Wait, wait, wait!" I panted as I adjusted to the painful invasion of my body.

"Just give me a second, pleeeaasse!" I whined holding only the head of his cock inside me.

After a few seconds he put my ankles on the tops of his shoulders and leaned into me. His cock began its slow advance into my bottom, each thrust a little deeper than before.

"You like that don't you?" he whispered.

"Mmmmmm", was all that I could mutter, keenly aware that with each thrust I was taking more and more cock, deeper and deeper.

I was finally living my dream and it was everything I thought it would be and more. My hole eventually relaxed and Marcus' cock moved freely in and out of my bottom causing me to moan continually. I became increasingly horny as we fucked.

"I want to get in you raw", he moaned, reaching down for his cock, I immediately stopped him.

"If you can't use the condom you can't get in me".

I could sense his heightened excitement and knew we were about to engage in something primal, something dangerous, something sinful. He put his hand behind my head and pulled me forward to make me watch. I lost my breath and shook as he entered me; I was so loose now that he slid easily inside me. I could resist him no more. I didn't want to; I wanted everything he could give me!

He leaned into me, pushing my legs back further, his cock reaching unimaginable depths inside me. Our lips met and we kissed deeply. I took his tongue inside my mouth and held him close as he forced the last inch of his cock inside me. I let out a low, guttural, animal groan into his mouth as a very deep, very dull, throbbing pain washed over my belly. I sucked his tongue deeper into my mouth wanting to have as much of him as deep inside every part of me possible. Reacting to my moans he forcefully ground his hips against me, his nest of pubic hair grinding against my soft bottom, his cock buried up to the hilt. I moaned louder and he pushed harder, I tightened my muscles around his cock and tried to pull him inside further. He raised his head and let out a loud moan, in response to the tugging of my hole on his cock. He buried his tongue deeply into my mouth and we held each other tightly. Both of us moaning passionately. Locked together like two animals I worked the muscles inside my hole tighter and tighter, trying to milk this cock inside me. Each time I tightened, he moaned and pushed harder against me. His weight was crushing me as he folded me in half in his quest to bury his cock as far inside me as possible.

He began to shake in my arms totally lost in our coupling. I was unable to move under his enormous weight and focused all of my energy on kissing him deeply, holding his face in my hands, sucking on his tongue, clamping down on his cock with every fiber of my being. He was pushing so hard against me I thought my back would break; the dull ache was replaced by a deeper, more painful ache. I let out a long whine, but it never made it out of my chest as I had a mouthful of his tongue. I had lost all control of my bottom as it tried to expel his cock deep inside my body.

Then he froze his breathing ragged and fitful. Our mouths locked he was sucking the breath from me, his cock began to spasm deep inside me. He was beginning to cum, at the same time I felt my body fighting to reject him as I too realized at that moment I had started to cum. Marcus filled the condom with his seed while injecting his cock into the deepest confines of my body, me holding on for dear life as his cock drained itself of cum into the condom while in me.

Locked in his arms his cock jumped and quivered inside me.

"That's right, give me every drop, I want it all inside me baby," I whispered to him.

Each thrust became less forceful than the previous, the torrid waves of cum became small spurts. Within a few minutes he was completely drained. I relaxed and enjoyed the "full" sensation that I had, knowing I took my first load and that it was a very big one. We lay together for another fifteen minutes as I gently caressed his hair and kissed him, thanking him for such an incredible experience.

Several moments later his softening cock slipped from my battered hole. We were one big, wet mess, but I felt great. He thanked me and wrapped the towel around his waist, headed out and closed the door behind him. I lay on the bed, never feeling more alive, the warm wet flow of lube, and my own fluids leaving my body. My bottom was completely numb. So this is what a slut feels like! I think I like this! In fact, I love this!

Marcus came back into the room and directed me into his bathroom where he washed my body. The feeling was awesome. As soon as I got out the bathroom I quickly got dressed and left for home.

This experience was the first time I ever willingly, fully submitted myself to a guy and it felt great. At that point I knew I was completely gay and all I wanted was men.

As the days passed I could not stop thinking about the sex with Marcus and I wanted more. I tried calling Marcus several times but he would not answer his phone. Days and weeks passed and he never answered. I often questioned myself why. Only then I realize that Marcus took advantage of me. He played with my mind, making me feel like he liked me and wanted to be with me, when all he wanted was to fuck my ass. Even after this realization, I still wanted him.

The best room service

I was scheduled to take a two-day business trip for my company to attend a business conference. I was really excited because I enjoy travelling. I left for the airport early the morning and got on the plane which made a stop in Barbados before leaving for Gatwick, England. It was very cold and passport and customs lines were disgorged into the cold and busy immigration hall at Gatwick Airport. I wanted nothing more than a cigarette, a scotch on the rocks, a hot shower and eight hours of sleep before I did anything else.

A taxi, organized by the conference committee picked me up at the airport and took me to my hotel. The taxi parked at the entrance of the hotel and I got out, grabbed my bags and walked inside. I wasn't surprised to see the lobby deserted, as my flight was delayed for a few hours and we didn't arrive until 2 in the morning. I walked over to the front desk where I saw a striking young man sitting behind it. He was a little on the short side but you could tell that he had a well toned body under his uniform. It had been a while since I had sex with another man so the sight of a hot guy turned me on almost instantaneously. I could not help myself. I stared at his body as I walked towards him. His gleaming blue eyes looked up when I stopped at the desk.

"Can I help you sir?" he asked.

"Yes I have a reservation here."

NOBODY KNOWS

About ten minutes later he handed me the key and I set off to my room. I unlocked the door, went inside, threw my bags on the bed and decided to take a quick shower before heading to bed. I kicked off my shoes and quickly shed my clothes revealing my slim, toned, sexy body. I never really tried to stay in shape but somehow my body always stayed well toned. I looked into the mirror and noticed my brown eyes were slightly vacant, but after the day I had I guess they had a good reason to be.

I turned on the water and stepped into the shower letting the water run down my body washing away the sweat and dirt from the day. After a few minutes I heard a knock at the door so I shut off the water, put on a robe and went to see who it was. I opened the door slightly and peered outside to see the desk attendant, so I opened the door all the way and signaled for him to come in.

"You forgot a bag at the front desk" he said holding out his hand with the bag I got from purchasing items at the airport's duty free.

"Thank you," I said and I reached out to take the bag from him.

As I reached the loose knot I had done on the robe gave way causing the robe to open revealing my cock. The desk attendant looked down at it bewildered; as I quickly grabbed the robe and tied it shut again. He handed me my bag and left in a hurry without saying a word. I guess the sight of my seven and a half inch dick must have taken him off guard.

I shut the door and went to finish my shower before heading off to bed. The next day I attended the conference which bored the hell out of me and the fact that it was approximately 5 hours long didn't help either. I was tired and starved when I got back to the hotel. I quickly went up to my room and ordered room service. After half an hour there was a knock on the door. I got up and opened the door to see the desk attendant with a platter of what I had ordered. I stepped back to let him pass and he walked into the room to set the platter down on the coffee table. I couldn't help but stare at his ass as he had his back turned to me and I was so entranced by it that I didn't notice that he was turning around until he was almost face to face with me. I quickly diverted my eyes up to meet his but I knew he had seen where my eyes were directed. What he did next took me by surprise. He walked over to me, planted a huge kiss on my lips and said, "I'll be

41

back later for my tip" as he walked out the door leaving me slack jawed. When the reality of what had just happened finally hit I slowly closed my hotel room door which was open the whole time.

All evening I could not help but think about what had happened earlier that afternoon and what was possibly going to happen later that night. It was about 10:15 when I received a call from the front desk informing me that a visitor was coming up to my room. Before I could ask who it was the person at the front desk hung up the phone. I was confused because I knew I was not expecting anyone. It was then it hit me that he was about to come up to my room. I quickly stripped down and put on my robe and eagerly waited by the door for the knock. A few minutes later the knock came and I opened the door to see the desk attendant standing in the hallway in a tee-shirt, a pair of shorts and flip-flops. I opened the door all the way allowing him to enter. He walked over to the balcony door and opened it as I shut and locked my room door behind us.

"I saw you eying me when you walked into the hotel last night" he said as he turned to face me while leaning against the railing.

Feeling a little ashamed I replied saying "Well I couldn't help myself those muscles of yours were bulging out of your uniform".

"When I caught you staring at my ass today I knew you wanted to fuck me, I was so thankful for that especially after I saw what you are wielding down there last night" he said as he moved his arm from the railing to the front of my robe.

Before he could touch me I slapped his hands away. I could tell by the sudden look on his face that he felt humiliated just for a minute.

"What is your name?" He asked in a soft tone

"My name is Stevenson Cook, but you can call me Steve". I looked into his eyes and said "Now you can go ahead Steve".

First he took my dick in his hands stroking it through fabric of the robe before slipping his hand beneath. The feeling of a hand on my shaft for the first time in a while was exhilarating and in the rush I leaned closer and locked lips with him. We kissed for what seemed like an hour before we went back into the room. There I helped him take his shirt off as he kicked off his flip-flops. I slipped my hands in his shorts to find that he wasn't wearing any underwear below them.

Taking his shorts in both hands I quickly pulled them down to his ankles revealing his uncut, nine inch cock. "Suck it." He said as I looked up at him. I quickly obliged.

I licked and kissed the base of his cock then I pulled his foreskin away from the head and started licking the shaft. He put his hand on my shoulder and started gently thrusting his cock against my face. I took the hint and put the head of his shaft in my mouth. It felt so great that my dick began oozing my preliminary manly juices which ran down my legs leaving a trail. He moved his hand from my shoulder to the back of my head and started pushing my head further down his dick. His thrusting started picking up speed and I could tell his orgasm was getting closer. Sure enough he pulled his shaft out of my mouth and started shooting, spraying his load all over my face, neck and chest. I wiped the load off my face, stood up.

"Now it's my turn," he said.

He moved around me to the foot of the bed and bent over, pushing his ass out towards me. I stepped closer to him, put my index and middle fingers of my right hand in my mouth, covered them with saliva and massaged his hole before pushing them in. He moaned with the pleasure and pain of my fingers up his ass, in and out, opening up his desperate ass. I pulled my fingers out, leaned forward so my chest was on his back, pulled his head back so his ear was to my mouth and I whispered, "Now the fun really begins."

I put my hand on my cock and guided it to his hole before thrusting it in and I didn't stop until my whole shaft was in his hole. He leaned back and moaned as I began thrusting my cock into his ass. I stood back upright, grabbed onto both of his shoulders and began to thrust harder and harder.

"Oh yeah, your ass is so soft and tight" I said as he moaned in pleasure and pain.

I leaned over his back so my chest was flat against him. I reached for his hands which were tightly gripping the sheets and continued to thrust as hard as I could. I felt my climax coming and I shot my load deep in his ass with a few more thrusts, finishing with me pulling his head back for another deep kiss.

The rest of the night we lay naked with each other on my bed occasionally stroking each other. The next day I left London to return home. It was sad to have to leave him like that. But I guess we both understood that it was just a one night stand. I must say the time I spent at the hotel with my dick buried into Stevenson's ass was the best part of the entire trip.

Weekend at Michael's House!

After returning from my trip overseas I was lonely for some time. The memories of the wonderful sex at the hotel always reminded me of what I was missing. My body craved sex and little did I know my cravings were about to be satisfied.

I decided to visit my friend Michael in the countryside for weekend. Surprisingly, when I got to his house that evening he was not at home. Joel, his friend of several years was at the house awaiting my arrival. Joel was a tall and muscular guy with the lightest brown eyes I've ever seen and a perfect tan that made his light brown skin shine.

As I entered the house Joel walked up to me and said that Michael had stepped out for the day and will not be back until much latter. He continued to explain that Michael had asked him to stop by to let me in. I observed out of the corner of my eyes Joel seductively staring at my body as I walked by. He then followed me into the living room. Ever since I was introduced to Joel several months ago while visiting Michael, I had a serious crush on him. I found him to be very smart, humble and quite fuckable. The sight of him staring at me turned me on at once.

"Nice tent." he said to me in his heavenly voice.

"What?" I said after a while.

"Your cock's hard." he said.

"What?" I said trying to sound surprised, but he just smiled and led me out of the side door that led to the backyard football field.

The cold evening air stung my eyes and cheeks as we walked. He guided me across the field while making small talk. He led me under the bleachers on the far side of the field and he kissed me.

Joel was well-informed that I was gay, obviously.

"That was the best kiss I've ever had," I said.

"Thanks, you weren't so bad either! Now let's see what you've got to offer."

With that he dropped to his knees and began to unbutton my jeans, but I stopped him.

"I want to taste you first." I said.

"But I have had a crush on you since the first day I saw you. It's your eyes; they've always seemed to draw me in."

When he told me this I became weak. My crush had a crush on me. I nodded my head and told him that I'd wait. And so he unzipped my pants and slid them down my legs, the cold air on my bare leg sent chills down my spine. "Don't worry you'll be warm soon enough".

With that he took my hardening cock through the slit in my boxers and licked up and down the shaft. It felt like heaven.

"Ohhhh. You have a huge cock. I can't get all the way down with your boxers on." Joel said.

"Can I slip off you're boxers?" he asked.

"Yes, yes just don't stop!"

With his mouth off my cock and the cold air made me throb even harder. He slipped a finger in the waistband and slid the left side down but then I felt his hot breath on my waist and his warm mouth bit my boxers and tugged at them until they were at my ankles.

"That's better." he said as he took my cock back into his loving mouth and began to swivel his tongue around my cock head.

"You taste so good." he said as he sucked on my cock so lovingly and tenderly.

NOBODY KNOWS

The feeling of Joel's warm mouth over my dick excited my body to the point that my body began to tense up with anticipation.

"I'm gonna cum! Ooooohhhhhhhhhh shhhit!" I yelled and with that I blew my biggest load ever down his manly throat.

Once he was done drinking my sweet man-nectar he looked up at me and smiled with a droplet hanging from his chin, he moved up and went to kiss me but I stopped him and licked my cum off his chin, and kissed him. I let the cum move back and forth between our mouths as we kissed. "My turn", he said as he sat up and undid his pants. From the outline in his briefs, I could tell he hand a huge dick. He told me to lay down on my back. Even though we were outside next to the back yard football field and it was a cold evening I happily did as I was told. I guess the thrill and excitement of what was to come kept me going. He slid his briefs down perfect legs to his ankles and worked his feet free. I gaped at the size of his cock and not surprisingly it was extremely huge. When I say it was huge I mean it was ass stretching the size of a small pothole huge, it was like nine inches long and as wide as a beer can with a really big vein running down the entire length of his dick; hence the reason I nick name him Mr. Big Vein. I shook my head no, but he assured me that he would go easy on me.

He reached into the back pocket of his jeans and surprisingly pulled out a condom and a small pack of lube. He rolled the condom onto his dick and greased it all over. Joel then spread the cold fluid on my tight rosebud and he inserted a slick, lubed finger inside me. He continued to finger fuck me for about ten minutes, one finger and then another. After three fingers I couldn't take any more. My ass felt so empty when he took his fingers out, but it was quickly replaced by his throbbing dick. His head entered easily from all the wonderful work he did fingering my ass and the rest of his cock soon followed. He started off easy, with slow yet forceful thrusts. He continued to fuck me like this for about ten minutes the whole time focusing on my eyes, it would have gone on like this forever until I yelled at him "Fuck me harder, come on Joel just fuck me like I know you want to." with that he laid into my ass with all he had, he slammed me like there was no tomorrow.

After what seemed like an eternity, our bodies were covered in sweat and his cock expanded in my ass. It was sheer bliss. This was too much for me. I shot another load all over my chest and stomach. For the first time since he started to fuck me he spoke,

"I'm gonna cum! Oohhh ssshhiiit!"

With that he slammed all the way in me and let loose all the cream he had to offer. He then collapsed on top of me with his cock still shrinking in my ass.

We laid on the grass in each others arm for some time until our bodies recuperated. We then went back into the house. Michael didn't arrive yet and I was not too keen for him to come anytime soon. We decided to take a shower together. Once we got in the shower we began to play around. I began to get hard again with all the fooling around.

"It's my turn," I said as I dropped to my knees and began to play with his hardening dick.

I began to lick up and down his huge shaft, sucking really long and hard on the big vein. I then formed a ring under his cock head with my lips and slid my tongue back and forth under his shaft. I took his head into my mouth and began to give the best blow job I've ever given.

"I have to fuck you. Now get on your hands and knees." I ordered him.

Following my instructions he dropped on his hands and knees and stuck his ass up waiting for me to fuck him good.

I positioned myself behind him and slammed into him. He cried out in pain but I kept on going, he was going to pay for making me wait to fuck him. I drove in and out as fast as I thought I could go, with the warm water running over my body and his. But then I heard a voice scream "What the fuck is going on in there? Who's fucking in my bathroom?"

We froze as Michael walked into the bathroom.

"Joel, you got another one of my friends I see".

We all just laughed.

"Finish him off, just make sure and fuck him well, he is too rude" Michael said to me.

Michael left the shower and went into the bedroom. With that I pulled out and slammed into Joel as hard as I could and rode him like if my life depended on it. I looked down at Joel and saw that he was jacking himself off in rhythm with my thrusts. He was really enjoying it. I began to slam into Joel harder and harder as I can feel my orgasm coming.

"Ohhh yes "I shouted as I quickly pulled out my dick allowing my cum to fly all over the place with most of it ending up on Joel's back.

He fell to the tiled floor with a slight groan very well satisfied. We got up and rinsed off in the warm water which felt so good. My weekend at Michael's house remains unforgettable. It was just the type of weekend in the country side I needed.

David and I

My sex life was picking up; I got myself a boyfriend, David, who lived overseas. To keep the relationship going I decided to migrate. I migrated to a small island in the Caribbean where David lived. The experience was new and exciting but not as exciting as the sex. In the early stages of the relationship, I must admit, I had to teach David everything since he was not very experienced when it came to sex. He had a few sex partners in the past but none of them could compare to me. I came across as a professional in bed. I don't think it was because I had sex with several guys, but more to do with the amount of porn I watched over the years. However, as we grew older in the relationship the sex got better and better.

This is how it all began. I hooked up with David through a good friend of mine. He was visiting the country where I was residing at that time and other than our mutual friend, knew very few people. We spoke over the phone for quite some time before we actually met. We were both single, we both had been in a few casual relationships…in my case more like one night stands. However, we decided to give it a try and see if a relationship was possible.

David was a handsome, brown-eyed boy, about five feet nine inches tall with an eight-inch, uncut dick. His body was in great shape and he liked to show it off. He obviously took very good care of himself and had nice, smooth, flawless skin. He wore fitted jeans and very fashionable clothes.

It took us a few weeks talking on the phone before we meet at a hotel a friend of mine managed. I arrived first, at about 7 pm and proceeded to check into our suite. It had been a long, humid day so it was nice to be in the hotel, which was cool and welcoming. About an hour later, David arrived at the front desk and asked for me. The reception directed him to my room. We greeted each other with warm smiles, both of us pleased to finally meet each other in person and relieved that each thought the other looked great. David came in and sat down in the living room. I ordered some coffee from room service, but he chose a cool drink from the mini-bar.

We spoke for a couple of hours and became totally relaxed and comfortable with each other and later, we went to the restaurant for a late dinner. Throughout the meal, you could almost taste our desire for each other in the air. It was time for us to get down to 'business'!

Returning to our suite, I put on a bathrobe suggested that he do the same in order to make ourselves more comfortable by getting out of our dusty city clothes. I then said that I was going to take a bath and I asked if he would like to join me. David hesitated, so I went in alone to fill the tub and add some scented bubble bath. I took off my robe and slipped into the warm bath. After getting into the tub and covering my hard-on with the soap bubbles, I called David into the bathroom to continue our conversation. I invited him to sit on the edge of the bath while we chatted. As sat down his robe fell open to expose his strong, muscular thighs. His eyes were shining; he looked so sexy that I placed a hand on his bare knee and started to run my fingers upwards. He placed his hand on top of mine. I gently pulled David towards me and kissed him. Our first kiss. It was gentle at first and then I felt his tongue against my lips. I opened my mouth and it darted in. The kiss became more passionate. I wanted him so badly. My legs were moving in the water so that my hard-on was no longer hidden from sight.

I loosened his bathrobe and he slipped it off his shoulders. It fell to the floor and I pulled him down towards me again. He lost his balance and fell on top of me in the bath tub. Somehow I felt as though he deliberately did that. I observed that he was also hard. We kissed again, and tentatively, our hands started to move over our bodies. For a long time we kissed, tongue against tongue, lips against lips, hands stroking and caressing. I felt him hard against me and he could feel me hard against him. There was no need to rush things, the water was still warm and it felt so good just being together, holding each other so close. We stayed locked in our embrace until the water grew tepid. Then we stood up, drained the tub and turned on the shower to rinse off the soap suds.

After the shower, we dried each other with the huge, white fluffy towels provided by the hotel, and David picked me up in his arms and carried me into the bedroom. He laid me on the bed as I looked up into his eyes. God, he was a beautiful vision to behold. He sat down on the edge of the bed and just gazed at my entire body. Then his hands and tongue started to wander all over my body. He tasted and kissed me everywhere. He kissed my lips, neck and throat, and he licked and sucked my nipples. I moaned with pleasure. When I couldn't stand it anymore, I got up, pushed him onto the bed as I began making love to his body all over.

My tongue traced a line down his flat stomach until I found his cock, which was rock hard and oozing with pre-cum. I pumped it a little to prime the pre-cum to flow, then I licked it off as a moan escaped from his mouth. I was enjoying the taste of his wonderful eight-inch dick. I wanted the entire length in my mouth so, in an attempt to get it all I took his hands and placed it behind my head and that give him the ok to fuck my mouth. David ran his dick in and out of my mouth as if he was fucking a well lubricated pussy. "Your turn," he whispered. So I lay on my back along side him. He kissed me passionately as his hands moved across my body, his lips traveled down from my mouth to my nipples again as he rediscovered just how much he could turn me on, by nibbling and biting them gently.

David then moved lower and found my hard, aching cock. After licking the head, he put it in his mouth. It felt good there and he tried to swallow all of it into his mouth but he was unable to. I guess this was the first time he had tried deep-throating such a big dick. He would soon learn how to with practice. I could tell he really enjoyed sucking my dick because his moans were louder than mine at times.

I turned my body into a sixty-nine position on the bed allowing us to be able to suck each other's cocks at the same time. David turned on his side next to me and found he could fuck my mouth easier that way. It felt so good. I loved how his hard cock entered then pulled out of my mouth. He asked me to do the same to him. I was gentle, not forcing all my cock down his throat. After a while, he wanted to experience more. "I want you to really fuck me in the ass" he whispered. I laid him back on the bed and lubed my cock while he began lubricating his ass. I put on a condom and immediately grabbed a hold of his legs. The sweet fragrance of sex filled the room. I took his legs and placed them over my shoulders and pulled him towards me, my cock directly facing the crack of his ass. Without any warning, the desperate David grabbed my ass cheeks and pulled me into him. The sensation of his tight ass around my hard cock felt really good as I began to move my hips back and forth developing a steady rhythm. I was fucking David's ass so hard and he was enjoying every minute of it. I felt him pulling my ass harder and harder into him so that he can feel the entire length of my dick deep inside him. It was not long before I felt my orgasm building. The moaning increased and suddenly I was cumming, filling the condom with my load. It felt great.

Afterwards, we relaxed together, stroking and cuddling, kissing tenderly. Not long after, I felt my desire returning and started to move around on him. I knew the time had come for me to show him what a good fuck was. I turned him over onto his hands and knees, doggy style.

He became very excited, as my tongue and lips moved across his back. I told him to hug the pillow and stick his butt in the air which left his balls and dick exposed for my pleasure. I licked his balls then sucked on them like a child sucking on a lollipop. I reached under, grabbed his hard, throbbing cock and pulled it between his legs so that I could suck it. I then buried my nose into his butt crack. My tongue licked across his dick as heated moans of desire escaped his lips.

At first, I was very gentle and slow with him, however, something about David told me he liked it ruff and deep inside. I began to direct the head of my dick towards his ass. Yet again he grabbed my ass and pulled me into him. I heard his moans; first from the pain and then desire as he felt his sphincter being stretched to receive my cock. It was all in. I waited a moment for him to get accustomed to the intrusion. Then slowly and gently, I pulled out of his ass almost completely and then slammed right back in. I started to fuck him hard and fast. He got really excited. He stretched out flat on the bed so I was lying on top of him; our bodies were held together by my cock being buried deep inside his wonderful ass.

David then asked me to pull out so we could change positions. He put me on my back and straddled my cock facing me so that he could ride me. He moved up and down on my cock like a man possessed. He was out of control. I was ready to cum when I heard his breathing increase. He cried out and suddenly I felt his sphincter contract around my cock. I sprayed jets of thick cum into him and at the same time, he came all over my chest.

Exhausted, he lay on my chest and we fell asleep in each other's arms, my cock was still semi-hard inside of him. A good while later he kissed me awake and rolled off of me. My cock plopped out of his hole. We both had dried cum on us so we got up, showered and went right back to sleep that night nestled in each other's arms.

My relationship with David lasted for just about a year. I eventually realized he was sleeping around and most of the things he told me about his life were all lies, if not everything. Nevertheless, I am grateful for the wonderful times we spent together that I can still write about it.

My consultant

After breaking up with David I relocated to my home country where I was faced with the horrid reality that I had to start my entire professional life over. It was a little depressing but I was ready to get back on my feet again and I started working on a few business ideas. I got myself a personal consultant and advisor to help me develop my ideas. I was twenty-three years old then and life was great. I was renting a wonderful apartment that had everything a bachelor could need or want.

The day began like any other. I got up early, had a warm bath which was followed by my usual cup of French Vanilla coffee. The only difference was my decision to work from home that day. I called up my consultant, Ian, and asked him to come over earlier as we had scheduled meeting for five in the afternoon at his office.

Ian and I had a really close relationship and we were both aware that the other was gay. Even though I found Ian to be very attractive and just being around him turned me on a great deal, he was much older than I was and I respected him far too much to even try a move.

Ian was thirty-nine years old with an eighteen year-old's muscular, sexy body. I could see he had spent years in the gym to develop his physique. His skin had a radiant and smooth appearance; there was no question about it, he took pride in taking care of himself.

It was about four-thirty when I heard my door bell ring. I was not surprise to see Ian handsome face through the peep-hole; he was always early for his appointments. He came in and we had a bit of small talk in the sitting room as we usually do before getting into business matters. It was getting really warm so I suggested that we go outside to get some fresh air. He agreed and we strolled in the back yard garden where there is a lovely swimming pool in the most beautiful environment.

We continued chatting for a while longer discussing general topics, nothing yet relating to business. As we stopped by the pool Ian asked out of the blue, "When would I get the opportunity to take a dip."

I looked at him and laughed, replying "Anytime you ready."

"Well, I am ready now!" Ian immediately said.

I had no problem with it and I thought to myself I would finally have the opportunity to get a glance at Ian's body, so I agreed and asked whether he needed to borrow a swim suit.

"No," he replied.

"I'm wearing them under my clothes. I am just wearing my usual briefs, if that is ok, I don't mind swimming in them," he added.

I was stunned; this could not have turned out any better even if I had planned it. We stripped, both watching each other as we did so.

"Well, I didn't know you worked out." he said startled at my lean, toned physique.

He was just as I had imagined; muscular, amazing abs and a chest to die for; his whole body had a sort of boyish charm about it.

He slowly slipped off his shorts to reveal tight blue and red briefs, gently bulging under the weight of his package. I could tell from the shape his cock made that he was uncut; I had become a pro at spotting the signs. There was a small point in his trunks where his foreskin probed the trunk lining with its taut pucker, while his tight balls hung beautifully shaped below. As I slipped my shorts off, I caught the look on Ian's face from the corner of my eye. He was obviously impressed with the bulge my cock made in my underwear.

As we walked around the pool to the deep end, I observed his package bouncing slightly with each step. I dived in, feeling the cool water around me; I could feel my balls clench as the water touched my skin. I swam under water to the other end and pulled myself out, sitting on the edge. Ian followed, pulling himself up next to me, our wet packages exposed by our wet underwear.

"Wow, I think I got some shrinkage just then, the water is so cold" said Ian.

"Did you?" I replied, and with that Ian leaned across and kissed me.

Locked with our lips together we ran our tongues into each other's mouths. The breathing got heavier, as I leaned forward pushing him backwards running my hands all over his sculpted body. Reaching down, I cupped his balls in his wet Speedos, feeling them sit heavily in my hand.

I was afraid that someone would possibly hear us so I suggested that we go into the house and into my bedroom. With our arms around each other we went straight into the bedroom and removed each others' wet underwear. For the first time since we've known each other, I saw Ian's thick, eight and a half inch dick.

Without wasting anytime Ian threw me onto the bed, slowly climbing on top of me, grabbing my dick and pushing it against his. He began to jerk us off together, and put his mouth close to mine, licking my lips. He then rolled of the bed backwards and walk towards my dressing table where he found a small black tube of lube Jelly.

"Are you ready?" he asked.

I just smiled and nodded, pushing my legs up into the air. He slowly walked toward me, piling the gel onto his fully erect cock, massaging it in, fingering the tip, and then, with the finger that was already lubed up, he began to stroke my hole. Deep moans were erupting from my mouth uncontrollably, sensations I had never felt before were flying through my body, but this was nothing compared to what was to come. Without warning, he thrust his index finger into my hole; a scream emerged from my lungs. He slowly pushed the finger in, wiggling it around, pulling it out, and forming a rhythm I was becoming accustomed to, until again, without warning, he shoved another finger to join his first. The feelings were intense, and I was hardly able to control myself. I was feeling as though I could have erupted already. I looked up at his face with its sexy smirk and grabbed his hair, pulling his face toward mine.

We were kissing passionately as he fingered my hole, and I loved it. After a few minutes, he pulled away from me, lubricating his dick some more, leaving me to watch. On finishing, he came back to me, pushing his tongue deep into my mouth, while grabbing both my hips, and for the first time Ian stuck his dick inside of me, all the way in, without hesitation. The pain was inconceivable, the burning sensation rising inside me. It felt like something were ripping me apart, but as the pain started to subside, immense feelings of pleasure replaced it. In and out, in and out he ran his dick developing a rhythm that I was beginning to really enjoy. Ian suddenly turned my entire body over, down flat on my stomach and then, again without notice starting to plunge into my ass deep and hard forming yet another rhythm while still passionately kissing me. Soon he was thrusting harder and faster, sending me into a frenzy of breathtaking pleasure and orgasm. After almost an hour and about five different positions, he finally yelled "Ohhhhhh, God, baby". I knew what was coming, so I lurched backward onto his cock, sending it right up inside me and just as his hot liquid filled my ass, I felt my dick shouting load after load of cum all over the bed at the same time. It was amazing. I could not ask for a better day of work at home, just me and my consultant.

Twice a charm

One Friday afternoon I received an unexpected phone call.

"Good afternoon, how are you doing?" said the caller in an extremely seductive voice.

Hmm, not another stalker, I said to myself. To my surprise it was Michael's friend, Joel. I was feeling a little awful because it had been months since we were last in contact after having such wonderful and memorable sex at Michael's house in the country.

"I am in the city for the week, a few representatives of my company are attending a seminar and I was wondering if you could show me around?" he asked.

I was all too happy for the opportunity to catch up and to have a chance to once again make love to him, so I agreed at once.

Just hearing Joel's voice was a turn on for me. I immediately asked him where he was staying and suggested that he stayed at my house. Unfortunately, he explained he was unable to as his company had already paid for hotel accommodations for him and a few other co workers attending the seminar. Later in the afternoon I went down to his hotel and picked him up. The look on his face told me that he was just as excited to see me as I was to see him.

I took Joel to dinner in one of the finest restaurants in the area and then invited him back to my house to hang out; he agreed. As soon as we arrived at the house and closed the door behind us Joel kissed me.

"I owed you that for such a wonderful dinner," He said.

I just simply smiled. Trying not to move too fast, I asked if he wanted to look at a movie or something but my PS2 was hooked up to the television because I was playing some games earlier in the day. He saw the game and said he would prefer to play the PS2 game. I did not mind so I turned the game on.

Joel and I played NBA 2003 on the PS2. Joel was real good at it but I wanted to spice things up a little.

"Hey. What if we made things interesting?" I asked.

"What things?" Joel asked with an apprehensive look on his face.

"Say, a bet over who wins?" I proposed.

"But I've crushed you, like, the past four times."

"Yeah, but what if I actually beat you this time?" I said.

He just laughed.

"Well, whatever. Okay. If I win, you have to give me fifty bucks."

I agreed, "Okay, but if I win, then you have to be my sex slave for the entire weekend."

His eyes widened in shock, but also in anticipation.

"Alright, but I change my mind. Same goes for me."

I smiled, bringing all of my skills to this game. One weekend of pure pleasure for me if I won was all I needed. We started a new game, and he was surprised that he couldn't make a basket in the first few seconds. I stole the ball from him, and shot it from the three-point line. I had made my first basket of the game. This was going to be too easy.

The fourth quarter came, and he was getting nervous. I was up one twelve to one oh six. He was pulling a lot of plays on me, but I knew every one of them. I made another basket. 114-106. I just had to wait. There were fourteen seconds left on the clock. I stalled as much as possible, counting down in my head. "Fine. You win," he said, and dropped the controller. The final buzzer rang. I had my victory.

"What do you want me to do?" he said, still shocked from his loss.

"Take off your clothes. You won't be needing them for the weekend." I replied.

"The whole weekend?" he protested, but he did it anyway.

His cock was already fully erect and that big vein that I could remember was throbbing. Me too, I had a raging hard-on.

"Follow me," I said, leading him upstairs.

I took two pairs of socks from my dresser and tied him to the bedposts with his arms legs wide apart in an 'X' shape. I lubed up his ass, and began to finger him very slowly. He screamed; he hadn't been expecting that. After a while I felt his ass relax and he started gyrating on my fingers. He was enjoying it. My cock was dripping with precum, and his was practically drooling.

"Suck me, bitch," I said, taking my dick up towards his mouth.

Sure enough, he sucked my cock as good as ever, taking my entire length into his mouth. It felt so good, I almost came right there and then, but I wanted to save it for his ass. I pulled away and his lips followed me. I backed away moving my body down between his widespread legs and then without warning shoved my saliva-lubed hard-on into his ass. I knew he loved it hard and I was about to give him it just the way he liked. He let out multiple moans of pleasure as I pumped in and out of him.

The feeling was so magnificent. As I developed my in and out fuck rhythm, I could tell that he had totally submitted himself to me and was enjoying every minute of it. Before long I felt my toes curling, my stomach tensed up and I knew my orgasm was drawing near. It was as if both our bodies became one. Joel began to moan louder as I started to fuck him even faster, harder and deeper. Suddenly I let out an amazingly loud moan as I felt my cock head spew out a huge amount of cum all the way inside him. Simultaneously Joel groaned, and let out a satisfied sigh as he too shot his heavy load all over his stomach and chest.

Leaving him tied to the bed, I got up and went to the armoire and took out a candle and lit it.

"No, please don't!" he begged.

"You'll like it, trust me," I said soothingly.

"No, don't," he continued, but I ignored him and waited for the wax to start melting.

I was erect again, so I straddled him again feeding him my cock. He began to suck like never before and I could tell he was still hungry for it.

All the while he was sucking my cock I was just waiting for the wax to liquefy. As the wax melted I took the candle and tilted it, allowing a few drops to fall onto his stomach. He screamed, but the sound was muffled by my cock, which was dangerously close to another orgasm. As more of the hot wax touched his skin he sucked harder even biting my dick at times and abruptly I shot my load into his mouth. He swallowed every drop. I leaned my face towards his and kissed him, attacking his mouth with my tongue. Only then I untied him and took him to the bathroom to wash his body as I kissed and licked him all over. After taking a long sexy bath together we returned to the bedroom, replaced the sheets and went to sleep locked in each other's arms, naked as we were born. We slept like babies.

I got up late the next morning, however Joel was still asleep. As usual, I awoke with a raging hard-on and having a handsome, sexy man in my bed I just had to give my hard cock what it was asking for...a sweet ass to fuck. Quietly, I took my dick and placed the head at the tip of Joel's asshole while he was still asleep. As I started to push forward Joel awoke. Knowing what was about to happen he pushed his body backwards in submission as I ran my dick up his ass. He began to moan out loud as he grabbed a hold of my ass pulling me into him. I could tell he really wanted it so I started to pump my dick deep inside of him without any remorse. To my surprise Joel begged for more and before long I was shooting my load all the way up his ass. I lay down on his body as I tried to recuperate, with my dick still inside his ass.

"Get me something to eat, slave. All that fucking made me hungry" I said, as I got off the bed and lead him downstairs to the kitchen.

I had Joel make breakfast as he was still under my control for the rest of the weekend. After breakfast we took a short swim in the pool in the back and although my body was tired and drained, I was still horny.

I went back to bed for a quick nap leaving Joel downstairs in the living room playing games on the PS2. When I eventually got up it was about six o'clock in the evening. And my cock was hard and rearing to go. Knowing that the weekend was not over I went to find to find my sex slave because I was a man in need. When I got downstairs to my great surprise Joel had dinner already prepared. As I was still hungry after the meal, I decided to have him for desert. I slowly removed his clothing, mine soon followed and we made out right there in the kitchen slipping down onto the cool, tiled floor. He pulled away a little and reached down and grabbed hold of my dick, gently rubbing it and sending shock waves of pure delight throughout my body.

I lay flat on my back and he moved in position to suck me off. I asked him if he was sure he wanted to do this again with fear that I would have hurt him, and he replied by swallowing most of my cock without hesitation. His natural athleticism and grace made him remarkable at performing a blow job, and he just knew how to most effectively pleasure me.

He sucked like a hungry man who had not eaten in weeks, his hands supporting him on the tiles. Up and down he went, his tongue performing miracles on my dick. In no time at all, he had me on the verge of cumming, so he pulled away and jerked me off faster and harder. Some of my cream shot straight up and hit him in his face, while the rest of it splattered onto my body.

This was heaven. Within the past 24 hours I had orgasmed three times. He stood up and grabbed some paper towels, passing them to me to wipe myself off, though we both were covered in cum. I don't think he was really ready for it again.

Quite suddenly, Joel turned me over and pinned me with my stomach to the floor, and held me there with his pre-cum lubricated dick pressed between my ass cheeks. He was getting harder by the minute, and I tried to turn around to face him, but he held me there. He whispered in my ear "it's my turn now, hope you ready for the ride".

I felt his hand slide down my back and rest on my ass, and then the arm that pinned me slid down to join it. He separated the cheeks and moved his dick toward my crack. I felt the head meet my hole, and counted to myself the seconds it took for him to start to enter. He pushed in slowly at first, entering my ass and proving his dominance over me. Oh, I loved it. I felt his cockhead enter, and then he quickly pushed all the way through. The feeling was He was then able to move back and forth easily, making me twitch with delight. He was a true professional. Harder and faster he began to go inside me. It had been a while since I got a good dick but I was taking it all even though the pain was unbearable.

He moved fasted and faster, his hands now on my hips holding me steady. His fingers gripped my hip, and I swear I felt his pubes brush my ass at one point. This was very notable as he was part of a swim team and he had recently shaved for the swim divisional. Before I knew what had happened, he had shot his load and his thrusts were slowing down as he finished pumping his warm cum into my willing ass. He slipped out, completely drained. What a fucking ride, I thought to myself. My ass was too sore to move so I laid back and we fell asleep in each other's arms, again.

The next morning we got up early because Joel had to leave and be back at the hotel soon before his co-workers started to get worried. Once again it was wonderful being in the company of Joel. The first time we had sex it was great and once again he did not disappoint. Doing it twice was really a charm.

Happy Birthday!

Every year I spend my birthday alone as I am usually either away from family and friends or most times I would rather be alone. This year was different. I awoke from my peaceful slumber with my arms still around Anthony, my warm body next to his feeling comfortable and safe. Memories of us making love the night before suddenly took over my mind; I was still amazed with his performance. He displayed a passion that I had never felt before. There was no other word to describe it but amazing.

At the time, I was away from home working on an assignment for my company. I was sent to the Caribbean where I would live for two years working and studying. As I was very familiar with the region and this island in particular, I found myself very comfortable and began making friends, easily. I was single and was in desperate need of finding someone. I decided to ask a close friend to introduce me to someone that he thought would be good for me. He introduced me to Anthony…three months before my birthday.

Anthony was a handsome, brown skinned guy with a low hair cut; pink, suckable lips and a tight, athletic body that could make any woman or man weak with lust. We hung out, toured the island and really got to know each other during those first few months. Anthony was very romantic and promised to make my birthday very special. He came over the night before and made love to me like it was the first time but what he had in store for me on my birthday was nothing less than the biggest surprise. Lying there, next to him, his naked skin against mine intoxicated my senses and I could tell I was falling in love. No longer did I care for what the future brought, I was too grateful that I had at last found Anthony. He was like a dream come true; someone to fill the void in me, to make me feel complete.

I felt the beating of his heart, heard his husky breathing, and smelled his wonderful fragrance as I lay in bed with him, my head resting against his massive chest as he slept. I stared at his face, relaxed and peaceful and wondered what filled his dreams; I wondered if there were thoughts of me or possibly the love that we made last night. Perhaps it's the delight of being in love and being able to express it freely. Whatever his dreams were my hope was that they involved me.

Suddenly, Anthony snorted in his sleep and involuntarily, I started laughing and shaking as I tried to stifle my mirth. However, my movement had already awoken him from his dreams and I shifted out of the way as his torso flexed as he stretched and yawned awake.

I was in complete awe once more of Anthony's hugeness and I gaped as the muscles on his massive frame flexed and quivered. Honestly, his power scared me, made me feel so small and weak next to him and yet something about that attracted me closer to him also. I drew from his strength - shared in his power. His arms were too large for my hands to encircle, he could have lifted me without effort, yet still he was so gentle, tender and loving.

His eyes opened and met mine. He lips parted in his wonderful, boyishly masculine smile, that implied mischief and shouts of love and my heart melted once more.

"Good morning baby boy, Happy Birthday" he whispered to me.

I grinned back, sticking my tongue out. He then reached over with one huge hand and tenderly tugged on my nose; reaching behind me with the other pulling my head to his as he gently placed a kiss on my lips.

After a moment lost in affection, we broke apart and I couldn't help but gaze at Anthony once more. His curly hair has ruffled, falling over his brow in messy strands. His piercing brown eyes shined through the glossy brown curls, boring into mine with laser-like intensity, going straight for the heart, finding my soul defenseless before its probing. There was nowhere I could hide my true feelings. I was completely in love.

Anthony sat up and the cover hiding his naked body fell away revealing God's wonderful creation. A gasp escaped my lips as I faced the glory of his naked form in full light yet again. As always, it was like seeing him for the first time. His body was so amazing. Anthony spent years on the wrestling mat and in the gym in order to develop what he had; a tall, broad frame with powerful, hulking muscles.

His strong arms reached out to me and pulled me towards him. I sat astride his massive thighs, sitting almost in his lap. Again he kissed me, with more passion than before. I could tell his lust was rising as the blood coursed through his body. If only he knew how happy I was to be in his arms, in his presence. My feelings for him were so strong; if he felt a small fraction of my love for him he would have indeed known what it was to feel divine love.

He then pulled me even closer, pressing his taut, muscular body against mine, wrapping his strong arms around me as his tongue probed ever deeper into my willing mouth, dancing with mine. His kiss was like no other. I felt dizzy, weak against the lust pouring from him. We broke for breath; his kisses always took my breath away and taking his hand in mine, I led him into the bathroom.

Anthony was so tall he towered above me. I turned on the tap allowing the water to flow before we entered the shower. The sound of the water reminded me of rain and how much I love to make love when the rain is falling. Sill holding my hands in his, we stepped through the door and under the cascading water.

The feel of the hot water being sprayed on my body made me shiver. I gasped and tensed and he laughed at me. His laugh was a warm husky sound free of care, but full of love. I found the soap and yet again took the lead. Beginning at his shoulders I lathered his wet skin, while caressing it gently with my fingers. I could not help my self as my eyes followed the streams of water down to his cock thickening responding to my touch. I just looked at him and smiled while I continued my task. I was unhurried as I knew I had him all to my self. He was not going anywhere. Anthony was mine.

I began to move downward, exploring the soft mass of hair between his Pecs. I washed his chest while feeling their thickness and mass. I rubbed down his body everywhere and massaged his pink nipples. Anthony gave out a deep groan of pleasure which was his way of telling me that I was doing a great job. I can recall glancing down seeing his enormous cock thickening and lengthening beyond its massive size as his passion increased.

The fragrance of the soap filled the bathroom, but it was the scent of love, passion and sex that filled the bathroom even more. Ensuring that I washed and cleaned every part of his wonderful body I then slid my hands between his thighs. I parted his legs then ran the soap up and down his inner thigh. He gasped as my touch sent waves of pleasure through his body. I knew he wanted me badly. It was my birthday and I wanted him to want me more than he ever wanted anyone else. My aim was to tease him in order to see how far he can go not giving in to his needs. How long was he going to remain passive as I excited him in every way? It was my day and I was determined to enjoy every minute of it.

I decided to take things to the next level and I grasped his large balls in my hand, squeezing gently while I looked into his eyes. He gasped.

"Please, suck me," he whispered hoarsely.

My eyes turned and faced his huge dick now pointing towards the sky. It was monstrously large, just about the same thickness as my wrist, with its trunk covered in thick black veins that throbbed and pulsed, like living snakes writhing over a marble column.

With one hand still squeezing his balls, my other clasped around the shaft of his cock, fingers far apart from meeting. I gently pulled it down towards my mouth, opening my lips wide to accommodate Anthony's monster cock. Hot spray washed over my face as I took the large purple head between my lips. The feeling was great. My heart rate instantaneously increased. I was just as horny as he was. I closed my eyes in ecstasy as his dick slid in and out of my mouth. Suddenly, he groaned aloud as he placed his hands around the back of my head pulling me forward as he pushed his dick further into my mouth, stretching my lips tight around his thick dick.

For a minute I though I was about to choke but then Anthony pulled out and rhythmically begin to fuck my mouth with his huge cock. The warm water running down my face made it even more difficult to breathe, nevertheless it made Anthony's dick slippery, helping it to enter into my mouth easier.

At this point my dick was rock hard and my body was in the throes of sheer pleasure. Anthony's breathing quickened as he fucked my mouth harder, ramming his massive dick deeper into my mouth, hitting the back of my throat with each thrust of his strong hips. My hand left his balls as I reached out to his huge thighs, trying to steadying myself by holding onto his muscular legs. I slithered my wet tongue over the swollen head of his cock and around the thick shaft as he fucked my mouth.

He then began rotating his hips as he fucked faster and faster, forcing my head back as he powered into my mouth, the veins on his cock pulsed and throbbed as they slid past my distended, tightly stretched lips. With his approaching orgasm his fantastic cock swelled to its full size. His dick forced my jaws to open even wider as he rammed into my mouth threatening to tear my lips apart with its huge width. Anthony moaned deliriously, the muscles on his arms flexing and bulging as he pulled my head onto his cock.

Suddenly, he stopped and pulled his dick out of my mouth. He teetered on the edge of orgasm, not wanting to satisfy his lust just yet. He then kneeled down beside me, kissing me his rock hard dick digging into my stomach, quivering with need. His breathing eventually slowed down, the gasping receded. Tenderly he picked me up in his huge arms as if I were no more than a mere child, carrying me back into the bedroom toward the bed.

I felt so great. My birthday was going wonderful, I could not ask for a better present. I felt so alive in Anthony's arms. The water on our bodies streamed over the both of us as he carried me in his arms. Tenderly he placed me on the bed and I remembered looking down seeing my hard cock pointing towards the ceiling. Leaning down over me, he engulfed my dick with his hot mouth, lips working over the swollen, purple head of my cock. With my cock sliding into his hungry mouth, he moved across to straddle my legs while his hands slid under my ass to find my wrinkled, tight asshole.

With his powerful yet gentle hands, Anthony spread apart the cheeks of my ass, as he supported himself over me on his elbows. Muscular fingers probed my tight asshole, massaging the tensed, tight orifice, wriggling against the opening, seeking entry to the hot flesh within. I was in heaven as my entire body craved for him.

While Anthony's fingers were probing my tight asshole his mouth was still at work. His soft lips encircled the straining purple head of my dick. His tongue gliding smoothly across as he teased the small slit before his throat opened to swallow me. Suddenly his throat tensed, squeezing the entire length of my cock, while his hot tongue licked the thick vein on the underside of the base, before he lifted his head, sliding my dick out for his tongue. Immediately he returned to my cock-slit, teasing me slowly to orgasm.

Anthony then breached my asshole as a finger slid into me with painful ecstasy. My entire body tensed with the raw pleasure. I remember feeling another finger sliding past the rings of clenched muscle. I screamed aloud as the skin of my asshole was stretched further by his fingers sliding up into me. My mind body and soul was being pushed into the deepest ecstasy I had ever felt as he finger fucked my ass with a steady rhythm.

With all the excitement I felt my orgasm approaching near. My orgasm rushed up into my dick like a vast flood heading to crash down into a river. My breathing became more erratic at this point. Suddenly Anthony stopped, removing his fingers abruptly from my ass, as he backed off. We were both sweating uncontrollably. I could remember seeing sweat glistening across his massive chest as he stared directly into my eyes. Anthony was teasing me and he was doing a really good job at it. He then began to kiss me tenderly and whispered in my ear "I love you baby. I have other plans for you, I am not ready for you to release just yet".

It took a while before my tension receded. We started to kiss again and a murmur of approval escaped my lips as my hands ran through his hair and down his broad back, feeling the hard ridges of muscle there bunch and swell with each move of his attractive head. Anthony began sucking my nipples. The suction increased as he moved from nipple to nipple, rolling the one not getting grazed by pearly teeth, between his thumb and forefinger; massaging and kneading the firm points, as he sent waves of pleasure through to my brain.

I then moved my body placing one of my hands on his broad, powerful chest; I motion for him to lie back on the bed, his erection towered over his etched stomach muscles like some obscenely thick weapon. I clasped my fist around the impressively thick cock, unable to get my large hand anywhere near closing around the solid shaft. I stroked the full length of his raging erection, feeling it harden further under my attentions, stiffening even more with every long, loving stroke. The memory of the ecstasy it gave when last it was buried deep within me made me sweat in anticipation. I would be sated soon enough; pleasure lay in other areas at the present time.

I then went onto my knees as I looked at the huge dick standing up before me. I took it into my hands and started to suck it. Anthony then placed his hands on either side of my head as he whispered reassurance; I concentrated and angled my head as he pushed my head back and forth. I relaxed and opened my throat in preparation for what was to come. He forced his massive cock into my mouth. The feeling was overwhelming. I signaled my readiness to have my mouth fucked. Without any time to waste Anthony began to fuck my mouth in slow steady rhythm, each time getting deeper and deeper. Finally, with the strength of his massive arms he pulled my head forward, towards his crotch and the choking thickness of his dick slid deep into my throat.

Anthony's breathing intensified as he drove his length into me. His bushy pubic hair brushed against my nose and lips, as the long shaft drove down my throat, thick hard veins rubbing against my tightly stretched lips fucking my mouth ever deeper. The pace quickened as his orgasm approached. Suddenly again he stopped; he paused, waiting for the burning desire to pass.

He sat up, got off the bed and opened the bedside cabinet. As I lay down on my stomach, legs slightly apart, he took out the condoms and lube and sat on both sides of my calves. I looked back and I saw the muscles in his arms and shoulders bunch with frightening size as he tore open the packet and carefully rolled the condom down his dick. Its immense size was both exciting and frightening at the same time. He then opened the tube of lube. He spread a copious amount in his hand rubbed it on his dick while caressing it affectionately with his fingers.

Anthony looked at me straight in my eyes and I knew that it was time. I turned back around and bent over spreading my ass cheeks with one hand and squeeze a large blob of lube into the crack with the other. Unexpectedly he then grasped my hips with my hands, pulling me up to kneel. I guessed he wanted to fuck me doggy style. He cupped the cheeks of my ass with his strong hands, running his thumbs along and into the crack, massaging the lube into me with great care. One thumb pressed against my hole, slipping easily inside, aided by the slippery gel. For about five minutes Anthony fucked my ass gently with his thumb.

When I thought that was it for the fingering, Anthony then placed his other thumb at my asshole. He began to press forcing the second thumb into my ass. The pain was severe; nevertheless, I bore the pain because I knew he had to do that to really loosen my ass in order to have accommodated his thickness. Satisfied with his efforts his hands returned to my hips as he edged forward. The huge, blunt head of his dick brush against my left ass-cheek as a guiding hand ran it up and down the slippery crack of my ass. My body was relaxed and ready. A deep groan escaped from my slavering lips as I whispered hoarsely to Anthony, the love of my life, "Fuck me baby."

His enormous cock head slid past my ass cheeks, pressing against my hole. At that moment all I was thinking to my self was I hope I could handle that dick inside me again. The night before Anthony took a long while before he could really get inside me. His dick is really huge and taking it required lots of patience. All my muscles had to be completely relaxed. At one point I started to panic, however the desperate desire to have Anthony make passionate love to me kept me from giving in. He drew his body closer into me as he began to really press that big knob against my ass until eventually, that big head dilated my sphincter, and found its way through. Anthony's hands clasped my hips and his mighty arms firmly pulled me back towards him. The pressure roused as he drove that dick slowly against the rings of muscle surrounding my anus. I felt the pain slowly build; a tearing feeling as the skin is stretched beyond its norm.

Anthony rotated his hips, circling his fat cock inside my ass. He began fucking gently, in and out and as the pleasure increased he began getting deeper into my ass more firmly. I felt the rings of muscle in my anus being stretched immensely as I fought the pain. We both were sweating profusely as the desperate need to satisfy each other became greater than ever. Through the first ten or fifteen minutes I really fought the urge to scream. Until, suddenly, something gave. With a smooth gliding thrust, his swollen head rammed into me, the thick trunk followed, tunneling deep into my hot moist bowels. The pain was automatically converted into the greatest pleasure I had ever felt in my entire life. I screamed, not because of pain. I screamed out of pleasure, the type of pleasure that could make a man sing from his heart.

With a fixed motion Anthony fucked my packed ass. The night before the sex was great. But today the sex was just incredible. I could tell he was really enjoying my tight guts stretched around his thick cock. I gasped and moaned in delight as his enormous dick is stuffed up my ass, feeling its great size as it filled every part of my being. Anthony leaned over me, his fingers found my nipples and he began teasing and squeezing them as he slid slowly into me, dredging deep into my butt, making me gasp as his fat cock pushed against my insides. In and out, in and out was the motion he developed and he went in deeper and harder pressing his hot, slick, sweaty body onto mine, sliding up and down me with every thrust of his thick muscular thighs. His large hands grasped my sides as he quickened his pace. He grunted with every deep, hard thrust.

He then reached down to my own hard, aching cock and grasped it tightly in his fist, stroking it in rhythm with the monster plowing its way deep into my guts. I heard him moan, squeezing hard as he slammed harder and faster inside of me, opening me deeper, probing the depths of my butt.

Just for a minute it seemed as though I could not see anything. All I remember seeing were vast sweeps of color racing past my eyes as he sent waves of pleasure through my entire body. The feeling of Anthony's monstrous cock plunging deep into me, plunging in and out of my ass, forced my mind into gibbering ecstasy; I had a weakness for Anthony's sweetness. His sweat dripped onto my back; groaning wildly, his chest heaved with effort as he fucked me wildly, fist pounding my dick. Suddenly, I felt an intense fire rush through me, a huge force swept together from every part of my body, shooting through my mind and dick as I came in a blinding wave of flame. It was the best orgasm I have ever felt in my life. At the same time I heard Anthony screaming as he rammed his full length hard into me, grinding his hips into my butt as his legs gave way and we crashed down onto the bed.

The fire continued to rage through my body as my cock spurted gouts of cum, shooting forth in thick jets from my dick and Anthony's heavy body spasmed wildly atop me as I felt his orgasm rip through his loins. His cock pulsed in my tight ass as he began shooting his hot cum into the rubbers. Suddenly I was hit by another blinding wave and everything went black as I screamed again and slipped into darkness. For me, that was the greatest sex I ever had.

I awoke in Anthony's lap, wrapped in his tender loving arms and as I opened my eyes, I see him smiling at me. He looked into my eyes and again said to me "Baby, I love you with all my heart. Happy birthday." It was the best birthday I ever had and I was glad to have shared it with Anthony.

A few months after I had to move back to my country because the project I was working on in the Caribbean had come to an end. Anthony and I unfortunately had to separate. I often question why all good things always come to an end. We communicated on the phone for several months after I left but you know how it goes, out of sight, out of mind. As time went by we both moved on. Nevertheless, every time my birthday comes around I can expect a call from Anthony to wish me a happy birthday and also a reminder of the wonderful time we had on my birthday and all the other times we had spent together.

Not so straight after all!

Again, I found myself single, unhappy, and unsure of myself and really did not know what I wanted out of a relationship or out of life. Added to that, when I moved back home I had to find a new apartment. Luckily, I became friends with a guy, Chris, a friend of a friend and we decided to be room mates, not long after. Thing were looking up.

One day, I came home from work early as the office was really stressful and it was one of those days where I just did not feel to do any work, so I left. As I got home that afternoon, I immediately began taking off my clothes as I made my way to my bedroom, thinking that my roommate wouldn't be home for at least a couple of hours. I had invited a friend over to join me but he decided to cancel at the last minute.

In my room, all I was thinking about was sex. My body was craving the touch, the smell, the taste of a sexy man, so I decided to watch a gay porn DVD because I had the place all to myself as I was not expecting Chris to be home for another two hours or so. I didn't want him to walk in on me, stark naked jerking my dick. That would just be crazy.

Chris knew I was gay and it didn't bother him at all. We were really good friends and he knew that I would never try to do anything to end our friendship. I respected him but little did I know I would loose control and forget what respect was. One afternoon we were sitting in the living room watching porn and getting drunk. Trying to increase the excitement I decided to put in one of my bisexual movies. Chris began jacking his semi-erect cock quickly because of the hot chick that was masturbating on screen. Chris was not gay at all, however it was nothing for Chris to jerk off in front of me. We have jerked off in front of each other several times before but only when we were both dunk.

Suddenly, the movie began showing two men kissing. I sat down close to Chris, never taking my eyes off of him, wanting to see his reaction to the movie. He never took his eyes off of the screen but had stopped jacking his cock. I was worried that I offended or disrespected him. I just sat there and continue looking at him waiting for his reaction.

To my surprise Chris' cock was now rock hard! The sight of the two guys kissing really turned him on. I moved closer to Chris until our thighs were touching and sat back, I took my rock hard cook in my hand and start jerking it off hard and fast. All the while wondered what he was thinking. All of a sudden, Chris took his hands and slowly grabbed my dick while his attention remained on the television set. I could not believe it. I was converting my straight friend. Ever since I have know Chris I always found him attractive. He is the type of guy you just felt like giving a fuck, with no strings attached, if you wanted. He was handsome, nice body and he had the charm of a prince. When he touched my dick I could have cum that very moment. He started to slowly jack my cock while his other hand pinched his nipples. I hesitantly moved my arm behind his head and slowly caressed his chest, pinching his other nipple, slowly making my way towards his cock.

After a while my breathing began to increase rapidly as the pleasure began to intensify. I grabbed Chris's cock firmly in my hands and began to jerk it off. I thought both of my heads were going to explode. His cock felt huge in my hand and I began to explore his crotch. He scooted forward a little bit, allowing me access to his asshole. This was weird and exciting at the same time. I decided to make the most of this situation and sucked my forefinger in mouth before placing it around Chris's tightly puckered asshole. I loved the feeling of my slick finger massaging and rubbing his manhole. I only wish that I could see it with my own eyes.

NOBODY KNOWS

I took my fingers and began caressing his bouncing balls, pulling and squeezing them tight, tickling them with my fingers and loving the feel of his egg shaped balls inside his smooth sac. We sat there for what seemed like at least twenty minutes just jacking each other off and touching each others when I decided to up the ante and leaned down and licked the head of Chris' dick. I thought this was going to be it, he would allow me to really make love to his body but, unfortunately, Christ snapped out of his daze and smacked me on the back of my head. "Hay man stop, what the fuck are you doing man? Sorry, but I don't know what got over me. I did not plan to ever do this and was not quite ready to go that far, ok? I'm not mad." and with that Chris stood up and went into his room. I felt so bad. I went too far I thought to myself.

Just about two minutes after Christ retuned to the living room and stood up in front of me, his cock still hard. He just looked into my eyes and said "I am sorry but we can't be doing this." I was speechless. He then walked away again. I watched his still hard cock bounce up and down and his ass flexed up and down until he closed his bedroom door. That was about three months ago. We continued looking at porn with each other but never touched each other again until that day when I got home from work early.

I was horny as hell and the movie I was looking at was a new one, I had not seen it before so it was even more exciting for me. I imagined having someone's hard cock slamming into my asshole. I was lying in my bed, my hands firmly on my dick, jerking it. I moaned with pleasure as the feeling of an orgasm drew near. I jerked harder and faster. I then took my left hand and lubricated one of my fingers with my saliva. I then inserted the finger into my ass while my other hand jerked my dick. The feeling was so great. I could feel my orgasm coming so I moaned out loud with pleasure. It was then I heard a noise by my door which was opened all the while. I turned around in complete panic at the unknown intruder who had been spying on me. It was Chris. I was embarrassed as hell. I began to apologize to him before I noticed that Chris had his cock out of his shorts and he was erect. It was rock hard and leaking pre-cum.

"How much did you see?" I asked him, slowly relaxing.

"Honestly, I only just came home, and when I passed your room you were just getting naked. I heard you moaning so I came in and to my surprise you were fingering your self and jerking."

He laughed and continued saying "You obviously didn't hear me so I decided to sneak in my room change my clothes and come take a look at you. It was quite entertaining."

Chris suddenly realized that his cock was still rock hard and outside of his shorts because he looked down, then looked at me, then turned bright red.

"Dude, I am so sorry if I have made you angry or something. I mean…well…I was so turned on and…well…I started to jack off. Don't be angry at me."

I just smiled at him and layed down on my bed. Chris entered the room and came onto the bed, next to me. I took his hands and direct it to my asshole. I guess he knew what I wanted and he was ready to give it to me. He slipped a finger into my ass and began to move it around inside the hole. That one finger was followed by another which was followed by a third finger.

Suddenly Chris moved his entire body onto the bed on top of me. His cock was only a few inches away from my asshole. I knew what was going to happen and couldn't wait. Chris pointed his cock towards my asshole and at the last second, shoved his cock inside of me. The length of his cock inside of me sent a striking pain throughout my body but in the matter of seconds that pain was converted into pleasure. He began ramming his dick deep inside me, moaning hysterically, just about ten minutes later, I felt him shoot the biggest load up my ass. I couldn't believe the sensations I was experiencing. I could feel his load filling my insides while my ass was milking his cock.

"Ohhhhh boy! That was so fucking good man! Wow, I can't believe what I have been missing. Your fucking ass feels incredible!" Chris screamed.

I didn't want his cock to leave my ass, it felt so good and I was so horny. When he finally pulled out I felt his cum pouring out of my ass and down my crack, creating a puddle of cum beneath me. I was satisfied and I was sure Chris was also. He looked into my eyes and placed a soft kiss on my lips and then said "thank you baby boy, you the hottest". From that day on Chris and I became secret lovers. It did not last for long though, because like most gay freshman, Chris was usually wild and was interested in trying different things. Eventually, Chris was sleeping around with several guys, something I can't deal with at all. We ultimately made a decision to separate in order to save our friendship. We have remained friends ever since.

It was only a dream

I woke up early one morning from a dream that had me completely astonished. I dreamed I was having sex with two of my dear friends and I was enjoying it. I never knew myself to be that type of person. I got out of my bed and called my friend John and told him about my dream.

"Boy you can't see you lacking sex. Come meet me in town; I want to take you somewhere," He said to me.

Without asking a question, I took a bath, got dressed and left the house.

My friend John was a little slut. He loved lots of men. I think he holds a world record for the most dicks one man can take in a day. He will have an orgy with twenty men and him being the only bottom. He was that freaky. I met John in the town and he took me for a walk in an area I had never been before. It seemed very deserted. I trusted John because we had been friends for several years so I was not afraid. John took me to a bath house. He said he usually go there whenever he was stressed. I did not understand why he would go to that house. Little did I know I was about to find out.

I was already feeling jittery when we pulled in to the parking lot. We went inside and John went to the counter and paid. I still did not know what the hell I was doing in that house. John then passed me a key and told me to remove all my clothing and put it into the locker. I was a little worried at that point but again, I trusted him.

"What are we going to do here?" I asked.

"We are going to get a good message"

I quickly got undressed, wrapped a towel around myself and followed John. We walked down the dark hallways of rooms. It was then I could hear the sound of men having sex.

"Do you know what they really do here?" John asked looking at me and smiling.

"I don't think I want to know," I replied in a very nervous tone.

John then looked at me, laughed and said "Don't worry yourself, you will be fine, just go and enjoy yourself," while directing me down the hall.

I made my way around through a video room area where there was some porn playing on the big screen but there was no one there. When I looked back John was nowhere in sight. I kept walking further into the building wondering where everyone was.

Finally, I found myself in a very dark room, where I could not see anything but I could definitely hear someone being fucked. This was just an open room, with no doors. As I walked in my eyes adjusted to the gloom and I began to see a little. I observed as group of really hunky-looking, sexy men standing around looking into one of the open cubicles. As I walked towards them I could hear that someone was really being fucked hard in that room. I stood just behind the guys looking in. To my surprise it was John.

He was pinned down on a bed by four men and one by one the others were fucking him. He was really enjoying it because as soon as one guy came out of him he was begging for another to go in. Suddenly I felt someone rubbing my dick through my towel. When I looked across it was a really handsome, dark-skin guy who was wearing only a towel just like all the other guys. I could tell that his dick was really huge because it stood up at attention underneath the towel. He placed his hands behind my head and kissed me. His kiss was very long and sweet.

He pulled off his towel so now his cock was in full view. It looked like it was about ten or eleven inches and very tick. He then pushed my body down. I knew he wanted me to get on my knees and suck him off so I did and I was enjoying it. I was sucking on the big head for a while then I slid the entire length into my mouth. He held the back of my head and ran his dick in and out of my mouth getting it all nice and wet with my saliva. I was licking his balls and licking his cock from top to bottom. One by one the group turned to watch me suck his cock and the men around me started touching me and rubbing their dicks on me. I knew then that I had no choice but to suck all those dripping cocks because I was not going anywhere until I did. They all surrounded me. While sucking one cock in my mouth I held two cocks in my hands jerking them. It was sheer pleasure. And I couldn't believe it but I was having the time of my life.

I can't remember how many guys were around me in total but all I know was I was feeling cocks all over my face. Everywhere I look was a dick waiting to be sucked. Suddenly another man made his way to get in front of me. He had a large cock probably eight inches and quite thick. He was rubbing his cock in front of me while I was sucking off another guy. Then he grabbed my head and pulled my mouth over to his cock. I sucked his cock while he called me a little bitch and started to tell everyone around that I was a little cock whore and he knew just what to do with me. Then he shoved his whole cock down my throat. He started fucking my mouth deep, plunging his thick rod all the way down my throat. The feeling was great. I never knew I would enjoy being used like a slut.

The guy then pulled me up and bent me over a table. It was then I became worried. Around me had approximately ten to fifteen men and they all had enormous dicks, how was I going to take them all? All of a sudden I felt a cold liquid on my ass. The guy was lubricating my ass. He then started to finger me with one, then two, then three, then four fingers, really stretching me wide open. Despite all the pain I was enjoying every minute of it and wanted more.

He finally removed his fingers and I looked back to see all the guys lining up. I couldn't believe I was about to get fucked by so many guys one after the next. I tried my best to relax my body on the table as the first guy came forward. I can feel his dick pressing against my ass. As the head entered he ran the entire length in smoothly and began to remove it very slowly. Just before he was about to pull all the way out he rammed the entire length back into my ass. That was all I needed to send me to the roof. I began to scream as the pain was so unbearable.

After about three minutes the pain was no more, it was endless pleasure.

The first guy then pulled his dick out of me and said to the other guys, "Ok you guy you can fuck that ass pussy good now, I just opened it up."

Rapidly they were all coming into me one after the next, after the next after the next, fucking my ass harder and harder, deeper and deeper as my welcoming ass openly received them all.

Suddenly, I felt a guy come inside of me. His body lay on top of mine with his dick inside of my ass. To my surprise it was the guy who had first kissed me.

"Hey baby boy, I hope they're not hurting you. I am here to make love to you now," he whispered in my ear.

He began to enter my ass slowly and the feeling was so sweet. As he entered my ass he began to caress my body all over. I was in heaven. His hands felt like feathers running all over my body. Of all the guys who fucked me already, he was the best.

I began to feel my orgasm drawing near and I guess he knew I was close because his pace increased. I closed my eyes as the feeling of pleasure intensified.

"Ohhhh yessss" I screamed as cum flew out of my dick.

The feeling was great. I felt the cum running down my legs and my eyes opened. It's then I realized I was still dreaming.

What's love got to do with it?

Have you ever met a guy that was so sweet you felt like you could just give him a good fuck as a thank you, with no strings attached? I am sure you have. Well I am no slut, never been and never will be but we all have our freaky desires, we have all craved for something or someone at onetime or another. The question I would like to propose is this, if you were given the opportunity to fulfill one of your sexual fantasies while you are in a relationship, bearing in mind that this desire does not include your lover, would you do it? Well I did and I don't regret it because love had nothing to do with it.

I was used to being around celebrities. Once of my closest friends, who for many years was like a sister to me is also an actress on a daytime soap opera and it was through her I met several wealthy and famous guys who were interested in me. Around that time I had a boyfriend and being the good guy I try to be, I was faithful, and wasn't interested in being with anyone else. Until I met Mr. Nice Guy.

I call him Mr. Nice Guy to protect his identity. Mr. Nice Guy was one of the most famous Latin American singers who, because of his talent and desire to achieve all his goals, was able to make it big in the entertainment industry. He had sold millions of records and was indeed and international superstar.

I was introduced to him in the summer of 2004 at the Latin America Music Festival. He was so handsome and charming just as he appeared on television. We immediately connected. That same evening he invited me back to his hotel for some drinks. How could I refuse such an invitation to be in the company of this celebrity and have a man pamper me for one night?

When I arrived at the hotel Mr. Nice Guy introduced me to several other celebrities who were visiting for the music festival. The evening was wonderful. At about 11pm I decided it was time for me to get home but Mr. Nice Guy insisted that I stay at the hotel. I refused because I knew my family would have been worried, however I did promise to hang with him the next day.

At about 7am the next day my phone rang and to my surprise it was Mr. Nice Guy.

"Hi, how was your rest?" he asked.

"It was great," I replied.

"I am sending a care to pick you up at once. I would like to have breakfast with you, and after we are taking a tour of the museum. I want you to spend the day with me because we leave tonight and I may never get this chance again. I am not taking no for an answer, so put on some clothes, the car will be there shortly."

I could not say anything. I just followed his instructions.

The car arrived and to my astonishment, Mr. Nice Guy was behind the wheel. It's not common for him to travel without his body guards but I guess that day he just wanted to feel free. We had breakfast back at the hotel and then left for the museum. After the museum we had lunch at an exclusive Spanish restaurant then went back to the hotel. It was around four in the afternoon, just enough time for Mr. Nice Guy to get himself ready for the airport. While packing, he walked up to me with a hand band and said to me "I want to give this to you, it's a friendship band that was given to me several years ago, I want you to have it because I want you to know where ever I am in the world, I will always be your friend and you will always be in my heart". His words were deep and I felt weak in the knees. Mr. Nice Guy then looked into my eyes and kissed me passionately on my lips. It completely caught me by surprise.

A million and one things ran through my mind all at once. First, I forgot I had a boyfriend then I could not help but think that this guy is one of the most famous Latin American singers in the world, every where he goes millions of girls scream his name...and he is gay. I could not believe it. It was not common knowledge that I was gay, but I guess he got insider information because what he did celebrities don't ever do, well, at least not the ones I've met.

Mr. Nice Guy continued to kiss me. We began removing each other's clothing. His scent...oh damn! The musky scent of his maleness turned me on. He was all man and I couldn't get enough of him. He was so sexy. I have seen him on his music videos, without a shirt but seeing him in real was so much better. His entire body was sexy and his sexual energy was like a magnet that just drew me in. I wanted him and I could tell he wanted me even more. The moisture of his lips and tongue intoxicated me like a fine wine preparing me for more of what was soon to come. The stubble of his beard, so rough against my skin, it awakened so many erotic sensations within me.

When we were both completely naked Mr. Nice guy took me over onto the bed. As we kissed I began to work my way down his neck, bathing his skin with my tongue so that I could enjoy the taste of his skin. His nipples hardened under my tongue and he moaned aloud as I sucked on them. I buried my face into his skin and held myself close against him. His throbbing manhood was leaking with anticipation. My nails lightly scraped along the length of his legs and I turned so that I was lying with my head towards his feet. His organ stood up before me. It throbbed with every beat of his heart. My hunger for it at that point was driving me crazy. My desire to pleasure him was incredible.

I started off licking his balls. I first took one, and then the other into my mouth. My mouth was filled as I rolled his balls around on my tongue. The sweat of the day tasted so good. I pulled at them as he groaned in pleasure. I let them fell from my lips but I continued to caress them with my tongue.

I was going crazy. I still could not come to terms with who I was in bed with and about to make love to. Not for a minute did I think about my boyfriend. All I could think about is fulfilling the dreams of his millions of fans around the world. Next I took my focus off his balls and began to work my way up to his dick. His cock was about seven and a half inches long but very thick. For a while I thought I could hear it calling out to me saying "suck me, suck me, suck me". I ran the tip of my nose along its length and at the same time, I felt him take my own cock into his mouth. I gasped with pleasure as I felt him engulf me. I focused on his hard, dripping cock in front of me. He was leaking like a broken faucet and his pre-cum gave off a sweet fragrance that filled the room. I just had to taste it. I licked up the pool of pre-cum that collected on his belly and I prepared to take him deep inside of me. I smiled as I heard the groans that escaped from him. My tongue and lips worked to coat his manhood with my saliva so that I was able to begin a full assault.

As his dick entered my mouth I just thought to myself, "Yes.....I am in heaven." I relaxed and felt his thick cockhead pushed past the muscles at the back of my throat. I smiled again as I felt the hair of his pubes push firmly against my lips. I backed off for an instant and then took him fully into my throat again while he was sucking furiously at my own cock. I knew from the beginning that this was not going to be one of my marathon sessions of passion. We were both so very close to spilling our seed. The sexual aroma and energy in the room was intense, our orgasm was moments away, but, to hold off on the inevitable, Mr. Nice guy pulled his dick out of my mouth and stopped sucking me.

A little again and I would have shot the biggest load into his mouth but I guess he wanted to take things to the next level and did not want to end it so quickly. He then came down and kissed me on my lips again, looking directly into my eyes.

"Can I make love to you? My body craves for you more than you know. I really want to feel inside you, beautiful. Can I?" he asked.

I could not believe it was going to happen, I thought it was a dream. But it was a dream, that was about to come through. In response to his question, I just looked into his eyes and kissed him, giving him my answer.

Mr. Nice Guy turned me over on the bed with my ass in the air. I saw him stretched over to the side table for a condom and lubrication. After putting on the condom and lubricating his dick my ass was next. He lubricated my ass, fingering me, shoving his index finger went all the way inside. The feeling was great. He then brought his body up close over mine, holding his dick as he directed it to my ass. I reached back and spread my ass cheeks apart in order for him to have full access. As the head entered shock waves ran through my body. The entire length of his cock followed. Mr. Nice Guy was completely inside of me and was grinding his cock deep in my ass. His pelvis was pressed up against my ass cheeks and is balls slapped my ass loudly as he fucked my love chute with his thick seven and a half inch dick. I moaned with each thrust and each twist into me, and I clenched my ass muscles around his cock to give him as much pleasure as possible.

After a few minutes Mr. Nice Guy turned me over on my back with my legs spread up and apart as he lay on top of me. My hands were sliding along the length of his back and cupping his muscular ass, feeling his muscles contracting with each maneuver. Our lips were connected in a deep, passionate kiss and our tongues probed each other's mouths.

"Your ass is so tight baby, I love it" he moaned, taking a pause between kisses.

"I love your cock up my ass" I whispered into his ear as I sucked on his earlobe.

I continued to work his ear, then neck, with my mouth and he moaned his approval.

"Oh, yeah, baby."

I continued to lick and suck his neck as he thrust his cock balls deep and I could feel every inch of his hard, throbbing cock.

"You like that, huh?" he asked.

"Mm-hmm," I moaned as we continued to grind ourselves together.

As he fucked me deep and hard, Mr. Nice Guy looked at me with an intense passionate stare. I was motionless, my legs still open and apart and I could feel my asshole wide open and hungry for him to pump more of his dick inside me. He engaged me in a deep tongue kiss, as his cock slid in and out of my lubed ass. He entered me until he could go no further and began taking long, deep strokes. He was moaning loudly in response to the pleasure his dick was receiving. We kissed hard and I told him how I loved the feeling of his dick inside of me.

His pace quickened and his breathing increased. He kissed me harder and I felt his ass muscles beginning to tighten. I grabbed his hips and pulled him deep into me as he took one long, last thrust into me, burying his cock deep into my rectum. Then he began to let out a loud, guttural sound as his cock expanded in my ass, unloading a wave of hot, thick cum into the condom. Each contraction of his dick was met by an attempt to deliver his seed deep inside of me. He collapsed his weight onto me and continued to slowly grind his still hard cock inside of me. This was more than I could tolerate - the stimulation to my prostate and the stimulation to my own dick caused my balls to send its own load of cum spraying between us.

After a few minutes of lying like this, motionless, he kissed me, and told me that I had just surrendered my manhood to him. I did not mind, he was incredible. After recuperating we both went into the bathroom and took a bath. I went to the airport with him and said my good-byes. His driver took me home after he departed and it was only then on the way back that I remembered I had a boyfriend. Mr. Nice Guy had a serious effect on me. It's not that I was in love with him; but I guess the excitement of having sex with a guy that every other woman on earth would like to sleep with drove me to the roof. Love really didn't have anything to do with it. It was just a fuck that I don't regret. Later that afternoon my boyfriend called me to find out how come he was unable to get in contact with me, I simply replied saying "I was just having the craziest time of my life". Mr. Nice Guy and I have remained friends and ever since have been in very good communication.

In the office

Since my return home I was able to successfully open a business which was doing quite well even though the economy was going through a crisis. To keep my staff focused and get the most out of them I have been gently reminding them that use of the internet for social networking is prohibited but for some months now, my friendly notes and reminders have been largely ignored.

One of my newest staff in particular, Lindon, a young, slim man, twenty two years of age, paid no attention to my rules. His desk was situated just outside my office and I can clearly see his computer from my office window; he always had this guilty look on his face. I am constantly reminding him that I was once like him and had to learn the hard way. He thought he was swift but I was determined to catch him and make an example out of him one day.

I am without a doubt certain that as soon as he gets the opportunity he goes on-line into some chat room, maybe telling young girls that he's rich and has a large penis. Anyway, regardless, whatever he's up to, he has been told not to, company rules. And so, with my aim to catch him I set up my video camera, in my office, with its beady lens trained on Lindon's desk. He often works late, and I think I may capture him misbehaving on film. My camera's a pretty good one with a powerful zoom. If Lindon was staying back in the office late in order to use the computers and phones for online dating, I was sure I will have all the proof I need to sack him.

The following afternoon, before leaving the office I took the video camera home with me to view it. I was not surprised, all my assumptions was true. I sat down in my room and reviewed all the taping. There was Lindon, sitting typing, alone in the building, and occasionally going into a shadowy corner with his mobile, no doubt for sex chat. After several minutes of the same, I was about to fast forward the tape, when a man appeared at the front door, and Lindon got up and let him in.

The individual looked as if he worked on a construction site. He was horribly plump, and covered with sweat, hairless and messy looking. They chatted briefly, and to my surprise the man pointed at my office. I wondered if he'd somehow spotted the concealed camera, but he hadn't. Lindon nodded and escort the man into my office. Now that they were in the office I could hear them very clear. I turned up the volume a little, not so loud that my room mate might hear from the other room.

"Sexy, get over that chair, now." The strange man said.

"Yes Sir," Lindon replied.

The next thing I saw, right in front of the camera had me in total shock. It was Lindon's bare bottom curved over the chair. Conceivably the man was going to spank him, but then the man's overweight, pale, spotty ass blocked my view, filling the whole screen. It took me a split second to comprehend what was taking place in my office. Suddenly all I could see is the fat shaky bum gyrating, tensing and pumping. I really couldn't see anything apart from that big horrifying bare bottom, but I could hear squeaking and slapping. I turned up the volume a little more and could now hear breathing and moaning, panting in time to the thrusts. After about ten seconds the man grunted once and his arse came so close to the lens that the camera lost focus. When the camera re-adjusted itself, the man had gone; he was on his way out, fastening his pants around his massive belly. Lindon was still bent over the chair with his pants down, his smooth cute pale bottom exposed to the camera. Once the man had gone, he got up and pulled up his trousers and returned to his desk. I could not help my self so I rewound the tape to watch again, just to check it, you understand. The man's bottom pumped twenty times. I watched it again, and paused the frame this time. I knelt near to my large television and looked closer. Sperm was running down Lindon's bare thighs.

When I was thinking that the issue was staff going on social network, this bigger issue I did not know how to handle. I began wondering just how many time have he bent over my desk for a man to fuck him. Not that the first recording was appealing to look at but nevertheless I was determined to set up the camera again the next day, to see if there would be any repeated performances.

I got home the following afternoon; my room mate was not in so as soon as I got in the house I turned on my television set. I had lot of work to do in preparation for a few meetings the next day so I had to organize my documents; however, I was not interested in that, I was hopeful that there would be something more entertaining on my video camera. I wired the camera to the television, and pressed rewind on the tape. I sat in my comfortable chair, and realized I had the beginnings of an erect penis in my suit trousers. I stroked the length gently with my fingertips, enjoying the tickling caress and then the camera rewind stopped. It was ready to play.

I pressed play on the camera and sat back in anticipation. The first twenty five minutes were a waste of tape, I fast forwarded, watching myself on screen as I grabbed my bag and departed from the office. Not much later the office supervisor left after me, leaving Lindon alone once again in the office building. He seemed to be actually working for once! Then, on fast forward, he dashed to the front door. Whoa there! I pressed stop on the remote, and rewound it a bit. I settled back, excited, and unfastened my belt buckle. I watched Lindon typing, and then walking to the door. He unlocked it, opened it. He spoke briefly to a man in the shadows outside. I couldn't see him clearly, but it didn't look like the fat man who had buggered Lindon's bottom the previous night. "Come in, for God's sake," I thought. "Do him. I want to see you fucking Lindon's naked bottom hard." I whispered to myself. The site of it excited me. I felt like I was looking at porn, the only difference being, I knew the main star.

Almost as if he'd heard me, the man came in. He stood waiting as Lindon locked the door again. I was correct it was indeed a different man. They chatted for a few minutes. I was unable to hear anything they were saying because they were not in my office where the camera was set up. I could only imagine, as I undid the zip of my pants. What were they talking about? I wondered. For a minute I began to think that the guy was just a friend and he stopped by because they were taking longer than I expected to get started.

Before long, Lindon directed the man over to his desk, and then I finally got a good look at the guy. He looked as if he was in his late thirties, quite athletic looking, possibly he is a business man or an office worker; he was wearing a fine looking suit. In all probability he could have done some work for Lindon in the past and stopped by for his pay. I came to that conclusion when I saw Lindon fished out his wallet and handed the man a large sum of money. From the view I was getting it could be more than one thousand. The man pocketed the payment. The two of them chatted briefly, and then Lindon shrugged, looked around, and pointed at my office. The man nodded. I could not believe it; he was paying guys to fuck him. My heart was racing with excitement as I began to pull my trousers down to mid thigh; groping my balls and rubbing my stiffening penis as Lindon lead the man through into my office, unaware of the secret camera filming him.

Now that they are in the office I could hear them.

"What position would you like it today bitch?" The man asked gruffly.

"Hmmm, I wonder," Lindon blushed.

"Is it okay if you do it to me on my back?" he asked.

"Anyhow you want it." The guy shrugged.

"Take your clothes off man; I don't have the entire evening to waste."

"Ya man, just give me a minute." Lindon replied, and began to strip for the man.

First he removed his white shirt revealing his smooth hairless chest beneath. I removed my underpants, now I was feeling the leather of the chair under my bared backside and against my large hairy balls. My dick was fully hard, thick, I wrapped my fingers around my shaft, and I started to masturbate my cock.

The sight of Lindon pulling down his pants on the screen turned me on. He bared that smooth cute little bottom, as the man began to also remove his clothing exposing his wonderful body. In comparison to the guy the day before, Lindon had hit the jackpot. This guy was strong and sexy. His body reminded me of a supermodel. He grew impatient waiting for sex, and grabbed Lindon by the throat, shoving him back firmly on my desk, holding him down with one big hand, and ripping off Lindon's pants with the other. He slapped Lindon's legs apart and stood between his thighs. My office light was off so the visual was not all that great. As it was the only light came through my office window from the glowing strips out in the staff area. The man spat on his hand and started rubbing his spit into Lindon's bottom, making him gasp as he shoved a thick rough finger inside him, poking him as he lay there nude apart from black socks. I could hear Lindon moan out as the guy continued running his finger in and out of his ass.

I could tell the man had enough and was ready to fuck his ass as he wanted it. He suddenly reached down revealing a very large penis, very thick and very long. I could not believe little Lindon was about to take all of that. The penis stood up at attention for the world to see. It look big strong and mighty. I am sure it has done and can do lots of damage. He began working his bulging cock into Lindon's tight little hole. Lindon gasped and bit his lower lip as the big cock pushed firmly against him, stretching him open, easing a little deeper, a little more, and then penetrating him, forcing its way inside him.

Seeing the look on Lindon's face made me feel sorry for him. He looked as if he was in serious pain. Lindon gasped out loud, arching his back, and the man held him down firmly, grinning as he shoved his bare cock deeper inside. Without any remorse the man put both of his hands on Lindon's bare shoulders and pulled him hard onto his shaft, driving the entire length into him. I was in total astonishment by what I was seeing. That guy looked as if he was ten or eleven inches long and could possible be about six inches thick. If someone was to ask me to describe it I would have to say he was mixed with horse. That just could not be normal.

I masturbated faster as the man buried his long manhood right to the hilt in my staff-member's naked bottom, pressing his hips hard against that cute bum. Then he began pumping, harder and harder, deeper and deeper as Lindon cried out. He cried out in pain but the expression I was seeing on his face was absolute pleasure. He was actually enjoying it. In a steady rhythm the man stabbed his huge cock in and out and in and out, holding Lindon down even harder on my desk.

"Ohhhh God, ohhh man your cock is so sweet, it's so big, it feels sooooo good!" Lindon cried out.

"Yeah, you love it up your tight ass right?" the guy asked.

"Yes Sir!" Lindon moaned as the man began fucking him harder.

The guy was fucking him so deep and hard he was literally losing his ten or eleven inch dick in Lindon's ass. Finally the man shuddered and with a long gasping breath he went still, his testicles pumping thick sperm along his huge fat dick to spill and spurt and ooze inside Lindon's nude body. He lay on top of Lindon motionless, enjoying his long orgasm, and Lindon humbly waited for the man's penis to finish draining into him as they both moaned passionately.

To my surprise, the man stood up with his dick still buried in Lindon's ass and began pumping deep into his ass again banging the last bit of cum inside Lindon's bare ass, getting the last enjoyment from his cock. This guy had stamina, he fucked Lindon's ass like a professional and I found him to be incredible. I personally would not mind paying him just to fuck me really good one day. After going for about five more minutes he stopped and finally he pulled out his dick which was covered with cum all over it. I could see the flood of his sperm dripping from that pink well-fucked bottom, dribbling over Lindon's bare cheeks and dripping onto the desk. The man shoved his big, naked cock back into his pants and fastened his fly, nodding with satisfaction.

The guy departed the office and Lindon got off the desk, put on his clothes and began wiping up the semen from my desk top with a paper roll, scrubbing and cleaning and checking that there was no evidence remaining. I smiled. I had all the evidence I needed to guarantee me at least one good orgasm in my office before I fire his ass.

I rewound the tape so I can look at it again as I jerked myself off. Looking at the stranger and Lindon having sex was so hot it did not take me long before I was letting off loads of cum all over the floor.

I had planned to confront Lindon the very next day but unfortunately, I had a late meeting with a business client that evening so I set up the camera again and hoped for another erotic performance. I stopped by the office later in the night to collect the camera. After collecting the camera I headed straight back to my apartment went into my room and set up the camera on the television. I rewound the tape and began watching it. As usual, Lindon worked alone, late in the office. From what I can see on his computer screen I guess he was probably chatting on a gay chat site. He made a few calls from the office phone and then, yes, at last, he heard a knock at the door. He went out of view for a minute as he answered the door.

Lindon entered my dark office, but I could not see the man he had brought with him, he stood out of shot giving instructions speaking softly. I only saw Lindon standing there, head bowed, as if being told off. Then he pulled down his pants. It was the first time I had glimpsed his penis, and it was about seven inches long. Not too thick not to thin, average and just right. He turned the chair round and bent over, but this time he bent over it facing the camera, so I couldn't see his little bottom. He gripped the edge of the seat and I saw his legs open. He was biting his lip nervously. I wondered why. Next I heard a swish and a crack and Lindon jumped, wincing, tears coming to his eyes straight away.

"One." He said.

The sound came again, and again he jumped, knuckles whitening as he gripped the chair hard in pain.

"Two."

I hit slow motion, and this time saw, just about, the blur as the cane descended hard onto his bare ass.

"Three."

I put it on normal speed for the rest, enjoying the scene, my cock hard in my pants. I unfastened my trousers and quickly pulled them down to my ankles, bare ass on the chair, my prick throbbing as I watched Lindon's face gasp and yelp and count aloud each stroke of the cane. I decided to rewind it, and give myself a firm wank, up and down the shaft, for each stroke of the cane.

NOBODY KNOWS

I looked closely at Lindon's face, eyes watering, mouth open, and I imagined I was jerking off into his mouth. He was given twenty strokes of the cane, and then the punisher finally came into view to give that sore bare bottom a pumping. The man was wearing a short beach pants and a white vest. The pants were already pulled down under his wrinkled, old bum, exposing huge, drooping testicles and a big cock, which he slapped Lindons' bottom with.

The old man pushed his penis into Lindon and began humping him fast, really drilling him, and in no time he spurted his cum in Lindon's naked bottom, and pulled out his cock. Next I got a good clear view of the man, as he continued spanking Lindons' bare bum, this time with his hand, really spanking it hard, his drooping old knob swaying around as he slapped that nude bottom over and over, and Lindon counted out loud each one, wincing and jerking on the chair as he was punished. The camera suddenly stopped. The tape was finished. Nothing could have upset me more. I was just getting into it and was really enjoying it.

The next day I got to the office late. I called Lindon into my office and asked him to close the door. I asked him if he had something to tell me. He said no. I just looked at him and smile. I then asked him to stop by my place that afternoon because I need to talk to him about a business proposition I had for him. I told him to be at my place for six in the evening, insisting that he don't show up late or he could lose the opportunity of a lifetime.

Lindon arrived at my apartment on time. I knew my room mate would be out for the night so I put in the tape and as soon as the door bell ran I pressed play and open the door allowing Lindon to come in and sit in the living room with him. Immediately he observed what was on the television screen and I can tell on his face that he was totally shocked. He began to sweat uncontrollably as he looked at me, lost for words. I just looked at him and smiled. I then turned off the tape and asked him what exactly have been going on in my office after working hours. He began to stutter as he searched for an explanation.

Before he could utter a word I told him to relax. I have a proposition for him. I told him that after seeing the tapes I wonder what it would be like to have sex with him like the other guys did. He just looked at me surprise and afraid at the same time. I then proposed to him that if he had sex with me I will not report it to the police; however he will still lose his job. And if he refused I told him he would not only be arrested but also he will be out of a job and his reputation will be at stake.

I did not have to say another word, Lindon turned and looked at me.

"Time, location. I am ready anytime you are." He asked.

I just laughed to myself…hos will do anything to get their ass out of trouble. "Right now, right here, I'm ready," was all I said.

I told him to remove all his clothes and he obeyed my every command at once. I told him to get on his knees as I removed all my clothes. There wasn't any time to be gentle. I grabbed his head and stuck my dick into his mouth and started fucking his face with quick, violent thrusts. He could hardly breathe but I knew to myself he loved every minute of it. About ten minutes later I unloaded down his throat, making the strangest noises as I tried not to let loose with my usual scream of pleasure. Lindon drank every drop cleaning my cock head clean of any remaining cum.

I then told him to bend over, in a standing position. He was much shorter than I am so when I stuck my dick inside him it went all the way up. Bent over, I could tell he knew exactly what to expect as he began to position and brace himself for a rough ride. Without any remorse or sympathy I rammed my entire eight inches into his ass and began ramming it home like it was the last time I would ever have sex. He cried out in pain and began to moan loudly and to my surprise, he started begging for it. I fucked him mercilessly and we both enjoyed every minute of it. Before long I was cumming deep in his ass. He could feel me shooting and immediately started to jerk off his dick. Before I knew it he was also cumming all over the floor. It felt good and I made him feel just like he loved, like a little slut. The next day Lindon came to the office only to collect his things and he left for good.

After having sex with Lindon I felt guilty and really thought that I needed to finally change and settle down with my life. I realized that life was too short to be playing games. I was ready to make a difference in my life. I was on a quest to find love.

Looking for Love

Love doesn't make the world go round. Love is what makes the ride worthwhile. - Franklin P. Jones

How many times have you met someone and determined within minutes that you were in love, only to discover it was just infatuation, lust or dementia? How do you know if the mere glance of a sexy looking guy will turn from infatuation to a stalking charge? How do you know if a friendship will turn into something more? When it comes to love, there is no way of being certain how a relationship will turn out. It is all a part of the learning process.

In the process of looking for love I had to define what love is. What is love? This is one of the most difficult questions to answer. Centuries have passed by, relationships have bloomed and faded and so has love. However, I don't think anyone can ever give an appropriate definition of love because we, as a world culture, have made love out to be complicated, mysterious, and indefinable.

Over the years I have been given the impression that to define love is near to impossible. Maybe I have developed a fear that if I define it, it would somehow be less influential, less impactful and less exciting. Maybe I enjoy the whole mystery of it. But is it really that complicated? Perhaps the complications surrounding love come from everything we add on to this powerful emotion. In my quest to find love I decided to drop all the baggage surrounding relationships and define exactly what it is I experience in the moment I think I am in love.

The first question I ask myself is what do I feel when I am in love with someone? For me the first step or first feeling is one of acceptance. Feeling completely comfortable with that person and having no particular desire to change them in anyway. When I am at the point of totally believing within myself that that person is perfectly fine the way he is for me I pose no conditions on whether I will love them or not. This for me is called unconditional love.

Acceptance is followed by appreciation. I have accepted him now I must appreciate him. It's when my focus is on what I like about this guy. I can look at him and feel this sweeping appreciation for who he is, entirely. His joy, his insights, his humor, his companionship, everything about him, I will appreciate. When I truly believe I am in love with someone I believe that my appreciation is so enormous for this person that it consumes their every thought.

Failure to make your partner feel appreciated, results in the ending of several relationships. I have seen it quite a few times with a lot of my friends and their failed relationships. Love is the desire to make another feel good. We all want those we love to be pleased, secure, healthy, and fulfilled. We yearn for them to feel good in all ways, physically, mentally, emotionally and we must not leave out sexually, of course.

For me, love is an uncontrollable feeling and the expression of that feeling is through an action. This action could be spending quality time, giving gifts, an act of service or a physical touch. It is my opinion that one of the reasons why so many relationships fail is because the couple just do not express love adequately to and for one another. Most often it's an issue of time, or lack thereof. I have been in several relationships, as you may know by now, and most of them ended because the other party failed to give me the time I desired, even though sometimes, I must admit, I might have been a little unfair. Nonetheless, if that time was invested in the relationship I am sure the lifespan of the relationship might have been longer.

In examining what love means to me, I could not leave out attention. We all desire attention, whether we wish to admit or not. Growing up I came to realize that for me love is expressed when I was shown attention. There are many ways in which we pay attention to one another. We use our five senses. We use our ears to listen, showing our partner that we are completely present with them. With our eyes we look at each other showing undivided attention. Tasting and smelling connects you on a more sensory, intimate level. Touching, giving a hug, holding a hand, a caress, or sexual expression. We all need to remember however we express our love will determine the type of relationship have.

Falling in love is hard to predict. Unquestionably, we all have stories of unrequited love, broken hearts and dashed dreams of what could have been. Even today I am sometimes reminded by a smell, a voice, or even a memory of lovers and relationships that I wished could have lasted a lifetime. Now that I have grown to understand love up to a point, because as I've said, I don't think we can ever fully understand love, I have learnt that all relationships have to start somewhere. A friendship that becomes more, an infatuation that becomes a reality, whatever it is, somewhere along the line we have all been in lust, infatuation and hopefully love. But, by far the hardest one to define is how we know when we are at that point when we realize we truly love that person.

Over the years I have had several relationships, some lasting a month, some lasting months, some lasting years. At this point in my life I was determined to find love. I knew exactly what I was looking for but the problem would be if I am looking for it in the right places.

For many years I have been using the Internet as a means to meet people. Most of the guys I've had relationships with, I've met on-line and those relationships failed because I never took the time to get to know them in person. I met them only after chatting for a while and then automatically we became involved. It was as fast as typing 1…2….3….

During that period of my life heading online was actually the preferred method of hooking up with potential dates because it offered me more control over my dating pattern. I believe that I am in total control over the screening process. If I think I am getting along well with someone, great. If I am not, I move on. At the risk of sounding businesslike, it can be a lot more productive since I have such a busy life and spend most of my time on a computer anyway.

With so many gay dating sites out there I decided on a systematic method to selecting the site that is best for me and my method to go about finding the right guy. Firstly, I checked out a mainstream site as the larger sites are well-established and have a larger pool of members which increases your chances of meeting a partner. I would then screen posted profiles before joining the site just to ensure that the site had guys of interest to me. I have learned over the years that most guys online are looking for one thing and one thing only, cyber sex. I must admit that I too, have had my fair share of that. However, it did not last long, you cum and they move on to their next client. Sexually fulfilling? Perhaps. Emotionally fulfilling? Not so much.

I can remember like it was yesterday, just last year to be honest, I met this guy online. Christopher was his name, or so he said. We would chat for hours. There was something about the way he wrote that was just passionate; I could tell he was a true lover-boy.

I was having a serious on-line love affair with someone who knew my soul as well as I did. It was a very frightening way to live. I would get up every morning and I can't function till I've checked my e-mail. I felt the rush each and every time I received a new message. The times there was no mail, I walked around in a stupor, like the world had just ended. I didn't know how to feel anymore, because I was so in l love with this man. I didn't know what it was like to touch this man, yet he has touched me a thousand times in my dreams.

I never thought this would have happened to me, it has though. I didn't know how to respond. The frightening part was I didn't even know whether he was messing with me or if he was serious. All I knew was the feeling I had inside was real and I was not about to give it up for anything.

It was amazing to me how we could type the same thoughts at the same exact time. I was drawn to this man like no other. He seemed too good to be true. There were so many thoughts going through my head about him, and us. I fell head over heels for him; and he did likewise, or so I thought. We physically just couldn't do without the other, without that connection online. Christopher sold himself to be a very sensitive, passionate, caring, considerate, loving man of high morals.

NOBODY KNOWS

As our online relationship developed we began engaging in cyber sex. One evening in particular, it was raining and I was not only lonely, but I was also very horny. I was online that evening, chatting with Christopher as we usually do. I began sharing with him how I was feeling at the moment and he asked if I wanted him to make love to me. I typed, I would love that. He then asked when and I replied...right now, he just laughed...well...LOL.

Just so you can get a mental image of Christopher, he was about six feet, very sexy athletic body, just about one hundred and seventy pounds, with black hair and light brown eyes. His dick measured approximately nine inches in length and from the pictures I have seen, it was very tick.

Christopher began typing messages to me in the most erotic tone saying in great detail what he was going to do to my body. He had a way with words and with every line he typed my body became more aroused by the sweet words of erotic pleasures that I was hoping to fulfill with him.

"I will come over to your home. Without knocking, I will open the unlocked door and walk right in. You were awaiting my arrival. As soon as I enter the room without saying a word to you I will begin by unbuttoning your shirt and kissing your neck and chest, working my hands down your body. I will stand to my feet taking your face into my hands kissing your mouth and face and neck and shoulders...like you have never been kissed before," he typed. He continued typing, "I will then undo your pants, slipping my fingers between your thighs, groping your balls."

My imagination began to run wild. I could just imagine holding on to him tightly as he completely undressed me, getting down to his knees to take my massive erection into his mouth. As he typed I began to remove all my clothes. He continued sending messages describing what he would be doing to my body. "I would suck your big dick while allowing my finger to massage your balls and your asshole. Making you feel like you are about to explode in your sweet fuck hole right there and then. I would remove my hands making your body crave for more. I will then take your hands leading you to the bed." By the time he start talking about taking me to the bed I was already so hot and horny I could feel the cum building up in my dick. I sat in front of my computer stroking my dick so hard; it was like my life depended on it.

Christopher continued typing, "I am going to fuck you baby, would you like that?" I replied, typing "yes, yes, yes". He continued describing what he would do next. "As we lay down on the bed, I will stroke your dick as I lay next to you. As I stroke, I can hear your moans. I then move on top of you, kissing your mouth. Again I lower myself along your body, licking your nakedness as I go downward. My kisses increase in intensity as I reach your open thighs and you let out a moan and your dick jerks in reflex as your body spasms, your back arching as I reach for your testicles."

The way Christopher described making love to me drove me up a wall. I had to remove my hands from my dick because I knew that I would be coming anytime. He went on to type "removing my hands from your dick I would take some lube in my hands and apply it to your tight sweet fuck hole. Very slowly I will insert one finger into your anus. With my finger buried deep in you, I will begin to slowly go in and out, in and out allowing your body to relax. As your body relaxes I will increase the pace getting you ready for what is next to come. The instant I remove my fingers from your tight butthole I will put your long slender legs straight up in the air. As I take a full view of your beautiful fuck hole primed for action". As soon as I read that message my body was so hot I typed to him, "Baby, you need to fuck me now because I want to come". Christopher replied with a message saying "Okay baby, well I guess you are ready. Without anytime to waste I take the head of my dick and slide it into your ass. My dick slides right in, feeling no resistance from you. Your hole takes me in all the way, as I can feel your inner muscles tighten down on my shaft. Honestly, I have never felt a tighter ass around my cock baby. I want to plunge further in and find that secret spot inside of you that will liberate all of the energy that has been building up since I met you. I put my hands on your shoulders, forcing your whole body down my shaft with each forward thrust I make. I can feel my dark curly pubic hair tickle that sensitive spot around your brown button hole."

At this point I knew I was about to come as I read the erotic messages he was typing to me. He continued, "Baby, now you can't get enough of me, I can hear you begging for more as your moans intensify. I take one of my hands, placing it under your ass lifting you to get my dick all the way in while I use my other hand to jerk your big dick. I am now fucking your ass mercilessly as I jerk your dick harder and harder. Your moaning increases twice as much as mine. I can feel the cum building up in my dick and I can feel the veins in your dick increase in size giving me the signal that you are about to come. In and out, in and out, I am banging that ass, going deeper and deeper. I can feel it coming. I am about to cum baby. Ohhhhhhhhhhhhhhhhh yessssssssssss." By the time I read the last word my cum was shooting all over the room. It was the best cyber sex experience I have ever had.

Christopher was like a dream come true in the cyber world. But something about him was too good to be true. He would make lots of promises, promises he never kept. For example, onetime he told me would visit me for my birthday. He e-mailed me all the information and when I went to the airport Christopher never came. My love for him was so strong I forgave him. That experience made me question his honesty. I decided to create a fake account online and sent him messages. Immediately he began to reply expressing how much he would like to get to know this mysterious person, unaware that it was me. He went as far as sending pictures that I thought he would only send to me. Even the name he gave was completely different name to the one he gave me. It was then I realized that I was being played. I eventually confronted him. He blocked me from his messenger and that was the last I heard of him.

The entire ordeal with Christopher was depressing. However, it did not stop me from chatting with several other guys, some becoming friends and others just online buddies. Overall nothing as sexual as the experiences with Christopher has ever materialized.

Out of the experience with Christopher, I learned several life changing lessons. Love is patient, love is kind. It does not envy, nor is it boastful and it is never proud. It rejoices over the evil and is the truth seeker. Love protects; preserves and hopes for the positive aspects of life. Always stand steadfast in love, not fall into it. It is like the dream of your object of affection coming true. Love can occur between two or more individuals. It bonds them and connects them in a unified link of trust, intimacy and interdependence. It enhances the relationship and comforts the soul. Love should be experienced and not just felt. The depth of love can not be measured. If you look at the relationship between a mother and a child, the mother loves the child unconditionally and it cannot be measured at all. A different dimension can be attained in any relationship with the magic of love. Love can be created. You just need to focus on the goodness of the other person. If this can be done easily, then you can also love easily. Most importantly, I learned that we all have some positive aspect in us, no matter how bad our deeds maybe.

As time went by I began dating several guys. First came Alvin, and then followed Jasson, whom I dated while I was dating Roland. Some people may want to call me a slut, but whatever. I was searching for love. While searching I realize that most guys were on games. For example, Roland sold himself to be a really nice guy. Even though his dick was really small and he was suffering with premature ejaculation and was never able to go the distance in bed; I still give him a chance and treated him with love and respect, even though I had my other men on the side. We spent very little time together because he said that he lived with his aunt and she doesn't like him leaving the house and coming back late as it had become so dangerous. From day one I thought he was a liar. Why would a twenty-one year old man have to answer to his aunt if he makes his own money and pays his own bills? Only to get the news from a friend that he was living with his boyfriend. For me, I was not going to allow myself to be hurt anymore so I decided to play the game too. It did not take long before I realized that games were not for me. I still felt incomplete and the burning desire for love grew.

After a while my loneliness increased and my burning desire to be loved and to love someone was so strong that I would fall into depression thinking about how lonely I was. It was the night of my birthday; my room mate invited me to join him and some friends at a club. I told him the only way I will go out is if my best friend Fefe would come with me. I called up Fefe, asking her to accompany me to the club with my room mate. She happily agreed to join us.

When we got to the club, Fefe and I decided to leave my room mate with his friends because we were not enjoying the environment. We left the club at about 11pm and walked down the street. It was a Friday evening so most of the clubs were open, and pumping. Fefe was very freaky, I guess that's why she is my friend, and she said to me, "Let's go to a gay club." Without asking a question I agreed and we began to walk down the street to a nearby gay club.

NOBODY KNOWS

As we entered the club I felt a sense of complete freedom. We got into the party mood right away and made our way to the main floor. I was on my third beer and I was already feeling wasted. We went over to the sitting area where I observed a young, handsome guy sitting by himself not too far across from me. I began telling Fefe how I think the guy was really handsome and how much I wish I could just go over and meet him. Every time I look over into his direction I saw that his eyes were on me.

"Why are you looking at me like that?" I asked him with an attempt to create small talk.

"Because you are looking at me," he replied.

"Is it because you see something you like?" I asked.

With a smile on his face he replied "Maybe."

We sat down and began talking. I found out his name was Akil, he was at the club alone and he was single. He spoke about his failed relationship and how, like me, he was seeking something serious. After talking for over an hour he took my hands and carried me to the dance flow. For a while I forgot that I was at the club with Fefe. She was too busy anyway, having a good time dancing with the few lesbians that were there at the club.

While dancing on the floor I could tell that he was a very romantic guy. The way he touched my body while dancing made me feel like I could just make love to him right there and then. As we danced my dick got erect and was pressing against my briefs. I was not sure if anyone else noticed the nightstick that was raging to break loose, but I didn't care. I was having a great time. He reached around and grabbed my ass, pulling me close up against him. I could feel that he too, was stiff as a steel rod. He had to be at least eight inches. My hands slid to his firm butt and I grabbed hold.

"Not here", he said.

I was breathing hard.

"Where, then?" I asked.

He held my hands again and took me back to the sitting area. I guess he did not want things to go too far and I totally agreed.

We sat and got to know each other, our life experiences, family, friends, likes and dislikes until it was time to leave. Fefe and I walked him to his car where we exchange phone numbers, took a photo together followed by a good night kiss that made me weak in the knees. I said to myself Akil is a keeper and I really wanted to get to know him better and hopefully develop something serious, meaningful and lasting.

The next morning I got up with a hang over, wondering what I did last night. All I could remember is I took a picture with a guy, so I took out my camera and when I saw the picture everything came back to me. Thank God I did not do anything stupid last night. I then called Akil to invite him to go with me to the movies and right away he agreed. We met about three in the afternoon at a cinema just walking distance from my home. While in the darkened movie theatre, we could not take our hands off each other and focused more on each other rather than the movie. After twenty minutes into the movie we decided to leave the cinema and go back to my place.

When we got to my apartment, we went straight into my room and continued where we left off at the movies. Our kissing was so passionate I could tell he was not going to stop there. We began to remove our clothes until we were both completely naked. For the first time I was able to see his entire body. He had a toned, athletic body. To complete his total package he sported a surprising ten-inch dick. And it was the thickest dick I have ever seen in my life. It was amazing and I knew that one day I would like to try taking it, but that day was definitely not the day.

We began making love to each other. Akil grabbed my shoulders pulling me to him and kissed me hard. I felt as though we were already committed to each other. I reached over and ran my fingers down his body, over every part of him before putting my fingers to his balls and tickling over them. He moaned loudly.

"I know I said I try not to rush into anything, but I want to make love to your body."

In the sexiest tone he replied, "No sex".

Not allowing him to say anymore I my lips went straight to his beautiful male organ. I was sucking Akil and his moaning told me that he loved it. I kept sucking faster and deeper until I got him all the way in my mouth, well, not all of him but most. I definitely can't manage putting that ten inch, thick dick all the way in my mouth. He moved his hips so that he was fucking my mouth over and over. My own cock was so hard; I nearly came without any help. Before long, he was moaning and he pulled out his dick spraying his thick cream all over my body and face. Once he stopped cumming, I thrust my own cock his way.

"Suck me," I said. He dropped to his knees and took me right into his mouth. He grabbed my hips and pushed me deeper into his mouth. I looked down, watching him take it in deep. That was all I could handle. I began to moan uncontrollably as he sucked harder and faster taking my dick all the way down his throat. I can feel the orgasm coming so I pulled my dick out and came all over his face. It was the best.

We went into the bathroom and washed each other off, got dressed and went for a walk. We spent over two hours walking and talking. The conversation was so deep that for a moment we both forgot how far away from my home we were. We sat in a park to rest on the way back and were able to share each other's experiences, dreams and desires. One thing was for certain, we both wanted the same thing at that point. And that one thing was love. Maybe it was my lust, or serious infatuation, but at that moment I felt that Akil was the guy I wanted to be with.

Is it love?

*There is only one happiness in life -- to love and to be loved -
George Sand, 1804-1876, French Novelist*

I already know what I was looking for in a relationship and what love meant to me, but why was I still confused about love? A few weeks after meeting Akil we made it official, we were officially "involved", together, in a relationship, one that we both hoped would last.

As we grow up to adulthood, we form our needs and wants mainly from our childhood experiences which are extremely personal for every one of us. Within a relationship, there is the added complication of a myriad of emotions that go with love. These emotions if not properly understood can be easily misunderstood. Hence the reason, after entering into the relationship with Akil I decided to do what most couples forget to do, that is, to develop a good friendship by learning and understanding each other. No relationship is perfect; they all grow and develop over a period of time. And nothing happens before its time.

During the months we have been together I must admit I have been insecure. I believe it is fair of me to say most people feel insecure in one way or another. Many of us don't know it, some of us do. Most people hide their insecurities in numerous ways. What most of us are unaware of is the fact that our insecurities can turn us into someone we are really not. In my case, often I will ask myself questions like.....I wonder if Akil is hiding stuff from me? Is he in love with me? Is he seeing someone else? My friends would usually say stuff like "If you have questions about him forget it, it's not going to last". I often listened to their comments and questioned myself if what they are saying is really the truth.

Fortunately the questions I have asked myself were answered. I realized that relationships are really very complex things. We build up a lifetime's worth of experiences and thoughts and expect to meet someone who will be compatible with our own unique take on the world forgetting that they are individuals themselves with their own unique views. It's no wonder that we run in to compatibility issues.

To avoid having compatibility issues both Akil and I decided to take things slow. To learn more about each other, become friends and convert that friendship into a true loving partnership. Looking back now I realize that in the process of building our relationship firstly we should have developed a friendship, nevertheless, while in the relationship we did take the time to develop a friendship and it was worth it. We hung out, did the everyday stuff, met each other's friends and family, learned about each other's background, likes and dislikes and modes in different environments. This entire period was difficult for me because being around Akil had me in constant heat. It took us two months after being in a relationship before we could have sex. I must admit that that was very difficult for me because I am quite sexually attracted to Akil so being around him was like therapy.

As I grew to learn about Akil more and more each day, I came to realize that he was a very kind, gentle and loving guy. He brought order to my life in many ways and together we built a solid foundation for our life together. He has never tried to own or overwhelm me. Our lives have never felt intertwined or entangled, instead we have walked side by side in a quest of achieving our goals as individuals and sharing our achievements as lovers. We were two free souls enjoying each other with love and mutual respect. Our lives have been parallel, and in perfect symmetry and balance, but never enmeshed.

The day we had sex was incredible. I had made several attempts to do it in the past but Akil having great self control, kept me in line. I remember a friend asked me one time if Akil and I had sex already. When I told him that we were waiting and Akil was not ready just yet his reply was "If he's not giving it to you, he's giving it to someone else." It is then I was reminded that a relationship is between two individuals, whether it is male or female, male and male, or female and female, its not between two individuals and friends. As soon as you allow a friend's un-wanted opinions to get involved it can fuck up the relationship.

It was only when we actually had sex I realized that Akil was only waiting for the right time. We could've had sex the very first day we met but I think the timing was very important. After we really got to know each other and understand that this is what we both wanted it happened, we truly connected in our minds, our bodies and our souls. It was not just sex, it was making passionate love.

It was a lonely week; I hadn't seen Akil for the week. He'd been working and from work, straight home. He lived about an hour and a half away from my home so it's difficult to see him every day. On the Thursday of that week I called him about 5:30 pm which is just about the time he would leave the office. He told me he was heading out after work. I found it strange.

"Where are you going?" I asked.

"I am going to visit my baby."

I just laughed. I began cleaning the already clean house so that it could be perfect for when he got here. I was not expecting him to come over to have sex even though I wished he would.

At about seven o'clock in the evening Akil arrived. I had already completed my cleaning but didn't yet take a bath. I went to have a quick shower and Akil showered after. When he got out of the bathroom I was already in bed with only my underwear on. He came and sat on the bed with the towel around him. The sweet fragrance of the soap that he used was lingering in the air. He looked at me and smiled. His smile said a million words that I just couldn't put together to form a sentence. I got up and just kissed him. His lips against mine felt like a feather passing on my lips and his kiss was so passionate it caused me to immediately become weak in the knees and my heart began to race. My dick was instantly erect as lust took over.

We gazed upon each other for what could be the hundred-thousandth time. We have seen each others' body and have touched each other all over, but we had never had sex. We really did not know what to expect. The anticipation of exploring his body once again and making love to him was present. I felt like we had never met and I wanted to search and discover every exposed square inch.

Embracing again, the heat from our skin inflamed our desire to get closer. We lay on the bed, him slightly over me as his hands ran down the length of my body, shoulder to thigh. His kisses became more insistent as the minutes passed by. Parting my lips with his tongue, we went deeper into each other. My hands kneaded his back and upper buttocks. I pulled him on top of me, wanting the pressure of his body against me. By then our hard cocks were trying to share the small space between our stomachs, wrestling for the best spot. He involuntarily moved his hips, grinding the hard organ into my abs, making me even harder. Minutes went by unnoticed as we tried to blend ourselves together.

Our faces were smeared with the wet passion from our mouths. Our body heat had generated the light coating of sweat that makes everything slide a little smoother. His fingers had found my nipples a couple of minutes before, making them stand out firm and proud. He began to move slowly as his mouth moved to my chest, sucking the hard points and licking everywhere. I ran my fingers over his head, pushing his hot mouth hard against my tight flesh. I never wanted him to stop. He continued down as my aching cock tingled against his chest as he continued the trip south, stopping to kiss, lick, and suck at my belly button.

Suddenly his hands moved to my thighs pushing my legs apart. My balls chilled as the exposed sweat evaporated and they pulled up tight below my straining cock. My leg felt the first drops of his cock as he rode my shinbone. He rose slightly, looked at my face and smiled. I raised my head to watch as he claimed his prize with his mouth.

Akil's lips slid up and down my shaft, his tongue twirled around the head. My cock became so hard it was almost painful, but at the same time it felt so good I could barely keep control. I guided his head with my hands, pulling and pushing his mouth along my hot flesh. I began to seep drops of clear fluid as my dick continued to pulse. He eagerly licked up every drop. His licking stopped and at that point he fully engulfed me his warm mouth. The suction was exquisite, his tongue delightful. I urged him to slow down a little. I didn't want to cum too soon.

I turned my body in the opposite direction giving myself the opportunity to also enjoy Akil's cock. We were now in the 69 position. I wrapped my hand around the base of his cock and stroked his balls out of their hiding place. My fingers tickled the clipped hair covering his sack. I began to suck him like my life depended on it. He tasted so wonderful. The harder I sucked him the harder he sucked me simultaneously. All this attention began to push us to the edge. Suddenly Akil stopped and we got up and began to kiss again.

We had previously made love to each other's body but never carried it further to sexual intercourse. I knew we've been trying to avoid it because we didn't want out relationship to be based on just sex so I was not sure at that point what to do. I asked myself, should I continue making love to him knowing that it will lead to sex or should I stop? I really did not know what to do. No longer could I think, my mind, body and soul were in great ecstasy; I felt like I had no control of what was about to happen next.

We snuggled together, feeling our bodies touch. Our hands strayed over each other, feeling the life within us. Our mouths are drawn together again and again, sharing our breath as we have shared our love. Our kiss was so passionate I really did not want to stop. I suddenly broke the kiss and leaned over to his ear.

"Are you ready?" I asked.

Akil looked into my eyes and said "Yes, I am ready".

I got off the bed and went into my closet and got a condom and lubrication. After putting on the condom and lubricating my dick and Akil's ass I was ready to finally join our bodies together, making us one.

Akil was already lying on his back so I got on the bed and placed his legs over my shoulders. I really enjoy making love facing my partner because I love to look into their eyes when making love to them. Probing easily into him, I inserted my dick head into his ass. Trying to control myself as it was only our first time, I glided in slowly. I felt my dick stretching his ass; I could tell he hadn't had sex in a while. His tight hole around my dick felt so great. I began moving slowly back out, he looked into my eyes as I looked into his and from that moment on we did not have to say a word to each other. Our eyes did all the communicating. I pushed back in all the way. The fullness he felt was fantastic, I could tell by the look on his face. I began my rhythm, moving in and out. Not too fast or too slow. My pace quickened a little. We were now breathing much deeper and faster, as we were getting more into the sex. I rubbed and pinched his nipples, adding to the already unbelievable feelings running through his entire body. The stimulation was almost overwhelming. My mind raced to take in every sensation from my feet to my head. I questioned myself again, "Is this love?" I was in total pleasure and the feeling I felt inside made me feel as though I loved him. My movements sped up. I was now getting close and I could tell he was also. I think because that was the first time in such a long while we were having sex and the pain was almost unbearable for him, I stopped and pulled out.

The love that I felt in my heart at that point assured me that Akil would be mine for a lifetime and I had nothing to rush. I wanted our sex to always be special so if it meant my having to stop and do it another time I would. I didn't want to hurt him in any way and I didn't want to see him in pain. We both lay on the bed kissing and began to stroke each other's dicks. We were both getting closer again. We didn't try to cum together. To me that only happens in fantasy land. Akil shouted out his orgasm, sending millions of tiny pieces of himself on my body. Not too long after I was ready to go. He knew by the low sounds coming from my chest that I was very close. He knew the pace of my orgasms as it was he that produced most of them. Within seconds I was there, falling into that familiar place where time stops and your mind is suspended. I'm not a religious person, but I thank God for the orgasm. We all know it can't be precisely described in written terms. It's way too complicated for words. Yes, I'm cumming; firing explosion after explosion of hot cum falling onto my chest. The feeling was amazing. The best orgasm ever, I thought to myself, unable to actually compare it to any other. He leaned over me, wetting his chest and stomach with my sperm. We kissed long and hard. I held him tightly against me, never wanting to give him up. After a few minutes we separated, but only long enough to move to the bathroom where we showered and cleaned up. Akil had to head home not too long after as he had work the next morning. Unfortunately he could not stay over and sleep with me that night. We would have drifted into sleep for the night, safe in each other's arms, knowing we would wake up the next morning together. I guess in time that will happen.

The only thing I missed during the love making with Akil is hearing three words come out of his mouth. The three words that some of you wait a week some wait a month and some wait years to hear. These three words are "I LOVE YOU". Since we began dating I can remember Akil saying to me once that he was very careful when it comes to saying I LOVE YOU. I can understand his saying that he is careful but I just couldn't understand why he can't say it to me, is it because he doesn't love me yet? Instead of saying I love you, he would say I really care about you.

Maybe he is just being like the typical male. Based on what I have experienced with most guys whom I have been around they all feel self-worth is based on how much responsibility they can take, but feel a loss of self-worth if they accept responsibility but then find themselves disappointing the people they care about. Maybe that is how Akil felt. Maybe part of his hesitation to say, "I love you," is because it played with his subconscious making him feel that by saying those three words he will be walking down the road to increasing responsibility with the next step being: "Let's live together," "Let's get married," "Let's adopt a child," "Let's buy a house." But you know what? What ever his reason for not saying it, in my heart I feel it, and I know that what I feel is real. There is an inexplicable connection between both of us, a connection of the heart. I can remember resting my head on Akil's chest and listening to his heart beat. I realize that it matches mine. I then said to myself we were made for each other (Well so I would like to believe). Akil have been a constant source of inspiration to me, in my life and in my work. He has brought me calm and joy, and a kind of serenity and balance. Even if our relationship doesn't last forever the time we spent together taught me some valuable lessons that have changed my life forever and for that I am grateful.

About the author

It is not easy to find happiness in ourselves, and it is not possible to find it elsewhere. - Agnes Repplier

Z. E. Arlea is the name I have given to myself to protect my identity. I am 24 years old and haven't yet found the strength to confront my parents about my sexuality. Because of this I wish to remain anonymous.

I am a young businessman, a writer, teacher and motivational speaker. I am currently the Managing Director of a Publishing company and have written several articles on business, culture, and lifestyle that have been featured in newspapers and magazines around the world.

At age nineteen, I had started my first business. At present I am involved in several business ventures internationally. At a young age I was privileged to travel to several countries around the world for which I give credit for my knowledge.

My dreams are to be able to touch other lives by sharing my experiences. I don't desire to be rich but I wish to be comfortable.

Most people are inspired by famous people, celebrities, politicians, their teachers or even their parents. I am inspired by innovation which starts with education and I believe in lifetime learning. The more innovative the world is I am inspired to advance myself, advance the way I think, the amount I do for me, the amount I do for others. I am also inspired by everyone and everything in and around me the reason being, because I grew up in a very communal and resourceful family who always reaffirmed that whatever you are looking for you have already found and that everything is somehow connected.

www.ingramcontent.com/pod-product-compliance
Lightning Source LLC
Chambersburg PA
CBHW060410290526
45791CB00002B/693